Hillbilly Jim

The Incredible Story
of a Wrestling Superstar

Hillbilly Jim

The Incredible Story
of a Wrestling Superstar

Gary P. West

Forewords by Hulk Hogan and Jimmy Hart

Acclaim Press
MORLEY, MISSOURI

Acclaim Press
— Your Next Great Book —

P.O. Box 238
Morley, MO 63767
(573) 472-9800
www.acclaimpress.com

Book Design: Rodney Atchley
Cover Design: M. Frene Melton

ISBN: 978-1-942613-49-7 / 1-942613-49-0
Library of Congress Control Number: 2016909992

First Printing 2016
Printed in the United States of America
10 9 8 7 6 5 4 3 2 1

This publication was produced using available information.
The publisher regrets it cannot assume responsibility for errors or omissions.

Contents

Foreword by Hulk Hogan. 6

Foreword by Jimmy Hart 8

Introduction. 10

Chapter One. 17

Chapter Two. 21

Chapter Three 25

Chapter Four 31

Chapter Five. 39

Chapter Six. 47

Chapter Seven 89

Chapter Eight. 97

Chapter Nine 103

Chapter Ten 109

Chapter Eleven. 117

Chapter Twelve 123

Chapter Thirteen. 193

Chapter Fourteen 201

Chapter Fifteen 211

Chapter Sixteen 217

Conclusion. 227

Epilogue by Hillbilly Jim 229

About the Author 231

Index 233

Foreword

M y first introduction to Jim Morris was by way of an 8x10 photo of him shown to me by Jimmy Hart. He said this guy is going to be a big star and went by the name of Harley Davidson.

Jimmy was right.

I wasn't sure who he was as we had no connection. The first time I met Jim was at a TV taping when he was sitting at ringside. Vince (McMahon) cooked it up where we'd have this gentle giant on the front row, and at first I wasn't sure how he was going to get involved in my business in the ring. When it all played out I just wanted to know what direction he'd be coming from into the ring.

I just remember when I first saw him how big and tall he was, but more than anything else was that 24-hour smile of his.

Jim arrived at a good time for me. He was instrumental in driving the entertainment side of the WWF and played a major part of the Hulkamania thing. I was at a point that I really needed to pull the switch on entertainment. I was just starting to figure it out and was now not afraid to make a fool of myself.

I didn't want to walk the plank or get on the high wire by myself, but when Hillbilly Jim came along I saw how over-animated he was and how he entertained the crowd. Because of him, I began to realize the crowd's reaction was more important than wrestling moves.

Hillbilly Jim taught me how to really entertain the fans. I watched him and he worked the crowd like no one else… he did that more than he wrestled.

It was Jim who straightened me up and pushed me out to the next level of entertainment. He showed me how to do it.

When it comes to professional wrestling, sometimes you might come in as a cowboy and go out as an Indian, but his Hillbilly Jim character was pretty much spot on. He was very capable and very ring-wise, and I knew if they left him alone he'd be a huge star.

He was a great draw wherever he wrestled, and I always liked being on the same card with him.

Jim is such a good person, and there's no way he could have ever wrestled as a bad guy even if he wanted to.

Hulk Hogan

Foreword

*I*n my life I've received thousands upon thousands of phone calls, but none have been more important to me than the one I got from Jim Morris back in 1983.

I had known Jim from our Memphis days when he wrestled in the area as Harley Davidson, but then he moved on to Vince McMahon's WWF. There, he had taken on the persona of Hillbilly Jim, and was on the verge of becoming one of pro wrestling's biggest stars.

I had been in the music business for years, singing with a '60s group called the Gentrys. You may have heard about one of our songs, "Keep on Dancin." It was a top tier song that gave our group the chance to tour the country and allowed me to become a performer...but never a wrestler. I say wrestler, because my entertainment experience made it possible for me to become associated with an old high school friend, Jerry "The King" Lawler, in his line of business… professional wrestling.

I was, an over-the-top, loud mouth manager of several wrestlers, when I first saw big Jim.

I've met a lot of people, but then you meet a person that leaves an everlasting impression you never forget…that was Jim.

He was one of those rubberneck guys…when he walks in the room, everyone jerked their heads around to look. Jim had the "it" factor—size, look, athletic ability and personality—the total package.

It was easy to see why the WWF wanted him. As big as Jim was, there were a few others even bigger, but they didn't have that personality and his ability to talk like he did.

He had the amazing ability to adjust to the character they gave him…Hillbilly Jim. God blessed him with a lot of success, in spite of the horrible knee injury he suffered fairly early in his career.

Stars like Jim Morris don't come along every day with that special thing. The Rock had it, and so did Stone Cold and the Hulk. As a real professional in the business, he was always on, even when he was feeling bad.

It has always been my job in the business to make myself a part of a match even when not in the ring. That's why when I became known as the "Mouth of the South" it was okay with me. My loud mouth and outlandish clothes opened lots of doors for me.

I never forgot what Dick Clark told me, "If you dress like you are in the audience, then one day you will be in the audience."

And now back to that phone call from Jim. He told me the WWF was trying to reach me, and that he had recommended me to Howard Finkle who was one of their big shots. Oh, I had gotten his call, but did not return it because I thought it was a joke. So when Jim called and told me I really need to call them, I did.

Of all the success I've had in the professional wrestling business, it is a result of that one phone call from Hillbilly Jim. He's been a good friend, not only in wrestling, but playing music together.

Over the years we have been good friends from a distance, but then a few years ago we were paired up to room together for several weeks while we filmed a reality TV show, called Legends House. That's where we got several of the old WWF guys together and did a reality show; Jim and I became even better friends.

Jimmy Hart

Introduction

I've been a fan of wrestling ever since I can remember. Yes, I guess I was at one time one of those pencil-neck geeks Jerry "The King" Lawler used to ramble on about after he had stomped an opponent into yesteryear back in the '80s. My vantage point of seeing most of those matches came through the technology of color television.

However, it was a 14-inch Admiral black and white that my family had back in 1952 that allowed me to really cut my teeth on wrestling.

Anyone will tell you that living in the '50s was definitely not what it is today when it came to sports. Seeing a sporting event was a rarity.

There were times if basketball was on it was the Minneapolis Lakers and their star, big George Miken, and football always seemed to be the Cleveland Browns and their star quarterback, Otto Graham. Baseball was a little better. In the late '50s, NBC would feature a Saturday Game of the week. The sportscasters were two Hall of Famers, Dizzy Dean and Pee Wee Reese.

Living in Elizabethtown, Kentucky, our television channels came out of Louisville, 35 miles north...and there were only two. WHAS was CBS and WAVE, NBC. ABC hadn't really arrived on the national scene at that time, at least not at my house.

Grainy pictures were common. And so, too, were those headache-rendering horizontal rotations.

As scarce as televised sporting events were, wrestling, believe it or not, had its share of exposure. At our house, when Friday and Saturday nights rolled around, there was a good chance wrestling would be a part of the programming. Almost always my mom and dad would invite family and friends over.

Back then at night when the TV was on, all of the other lights in the room were out. I'm not really sure when all of that changed back.

My grandmother would be there on occasion. She was my dad's mother, and lived with us part-time. She was into wrestling like no one I've ever known. From my position on the floor (the adults had all of the chairs and couch), I remember giggling when my grandmother blurted out with a few expletives because of what one of the bad guys was doing.

"Mama, don't talk like that," my dad would say. "They're not really hurting each other."

"Not hurting each other," I would yell. "They're killing each other… look at the blood."

It was the most entertaining hour in the history of black and white, and I couldn't wait to see it again.

Back in the day it was the bad guys, those who had absolutely no respect for the rules or their opponents, that brought the fans in. This aspect of the sport has never changed over the years.

I remember some of the good guys. My favorite was Antonio Rocca. He wrestled more with his bare feet, often slapping an opponent in the face with them, instead of his hands. The announcer would refer to those feet as "educated feet." I never understood then or now how your feet could become educated, but it seemed to work. He bounced around the ring as if it was a trampoline. He flew off the ropes, ducking under roundhouse swings that were meant to take him out. When he lost, which was seldom, it was because of unscrupulous tactics.

Another good guy was Vern Gagne. He was always about doing the right thing, eating healthy, and, above all, playing by the rules. I vividly recall Gagne doing a self-promotion in the middle of the ring after a match touting his "Vern Gagne Protein Power Pack" vitamins. Sneaking into the ring behind Gagne, but in view of the TV cameras, was one of the great villains of all-time, Dick "The Bruiser." Suddenly in a single motion he grabbed the jar of vitamins and cracked them over Gagne's head in Rowdy Roddy Piper style, rendering him motionless on the ring's canvas. The Bruiser, now with the microphone in hand yelled, "Yeah, this is what these Protein Power Pack's will do for you."

Kicking the out-of-it Gagne for good measure and throwing down the microphone, he was gone as quickly as he had appeared.

"Its time for a station break," the announcer said. "We'll be back."

I found out later in life that Dick "The Bruiser's" real name was William Fritz Afflis, and he had played football at Purdue and later for the Green Bay Packers. I could easily see why he changed his name for wrestling, but I'm not sure he was ever the most dangerous man in the world as he said he was.

The guru's of wrestling had accomplished exactly what they had set out to do without me even knowing it. I hated Dick "The Bruiser." And when they announced later that Vern Gagne and The Bruiser would be facing off in a couple of weeks, I couldn't wait.

As for the good guys, Gagne was probably an earlier Hulk Hogan, but on a more regional stage. There were several similarities.

Never was it fun to see two good guys against each other. Dull and boring are two words to describe such a match. Even the announcers had trouble with it, and for sure the need for a referee was zero. "Scientific wrestling" was how such a match was usually described. Like the "educated feet" thing, I never understood that either.

But before Gagne and Bruiser there were others.

Gino Garibaldi was another of the throwback good guys who was featured in lots of matches against evil. And so was Lou Thesz, one of the most popular wrestlers ever. He was a six-time world champion who rarely lost.

But oh my, those bad guys never seemed to go away. Wherever they wrestled they drew the biggest crowds. The TV cameras would show them coming into the ring, and the boos and jeers would drown-out what the announcers were describing.

At the head of the list was Gorgeous George. His mere presence meant sellout. The Baron Michele Leone, Wild Red Berry and "Classy" Freddie Blassie were three others in a long list of villains. It was reported that a match between Thesz and Leone resulted in wrestling first $100,000 gate in 1952.

Over the years I never went away from being a wrestling fan. It wasn't, however, until cable TV emerged that I could come across wrestling from all of those smaller promoters throughout America. But when the WWF became the driving force, wrestling was like a runaway freight train thundering past all of the signals.

I still marvel at the athletes of these larger-than-life men, and finding out that professional wrestling was in fact a show, there for the entertainment, was much like finding out about Santa Claus.

As for my grandmother, well it was really an oddity that I could never explain to her how our country propelled men to a moon landing. "It wasn't real," she said.

In the biggest paradox of all, in her mind the moon landing was fake and wrestling was real.

From the inception of the World Wrestling Federation, its acronym WWF came under some light scrutiny from another WWF, the World Wildlife Fund. For the first several years their opposition was more of a fly-like annoyance than anything else and came from just the U.S. No big deal.

However, over the years the complaint began to pick up steam. Led by the United Kingdom, more and more countries came on board and before long international lawyers took up the cause against Vince McMahon. Seeing that the wrestling WWF had in fact infringed on the wildlife WWF, the McMahon's tossed in the towel with a submission.

Millions and millions had been spent on marketing the letters. It was one of the most recognizable names in America. But in May 2002, the old WWF became the WWE, World Wrestling Entertainment.

It was not without controversy. Now for the first time professional wrestling officially said their sport was purely entertainment.

But there was a bright side to it all. No longer did the wrestlers have to go through each state's sports commission, where various licenses and fees had to be paid each time they came to town. Every state had a commission and doctor, so those jacked up costs would be eliminated.

In this book, the acronyms WWF and WWE will be used interchangeably, knowing that WWE is the legal, official name.

Hillbilly Jim

The Incredible Story
of a Wrestling Superstar

Chapter One

Brutus "The Barber" Beefcake had just clamped down a vicious headlock on WWF champion Hulk Hogan in the middle of the ring during the main event of a match in San Diego on February 25, 1985.

The villain Beefcake would resort to just about anything to win, and against the Hulkster he was leaving little to chance. That's why he had, as his manager that night, another no-good by the name of Luscious Johnny Valiant. The intent was to win at all costs, and as Hogan mightily struggled to break loose, Valiant positioned himself by climbing onto the rings apron, intent on doing his part in helping to do-in the Hulkster.

The fans in San Diego Sports Arena weren't having any part of it, and their screams quickly brought Hogan's manager that night rushing to Valiant's side of the ring to put a stop to any sort of skull-drudgery.

Hillbilly Jim, the Hulkster's protege' and trusted friend, was working the champion's corner, making sure his man, if he lost, lost fair and square.

Grabbing Valiant's leg in an effort to yank him loose from the ring's top rope and back on the floor where he belonged, the big Kentucky Hillbilly kept tugging. Hogan suddenly broke loose from Beefcake, and in one sweeping move hurled "The Barber" across the ring where he slammed into Valiant, who then propelled into Hillbilly Jim, knocking him to the concrete floor.

At first glance it was just another collision of huge bodies that takes place every night in this violent sport of professional wrestling. With Jim writhing in pain, the crowd was now at fever-pitch, not realizing the wrestler's injury was for real. Valiant's big boot, at full force, struck

Jim's kneecap, dislodging it and driving it four inches into his thigh while ripping apart tendons and blood vessels.

"I was supposed to catch Valiant," says Jim. "It was a 'spot' (a planned move) that had been choreographed earlier. Heck, I was just supposed to be a small part of it—outside the ring and all. I knew I was hurt. Even through my overalls I could see my kneecap was not where it was supposed to be. It was like an out-of-body experience."

The blow didn't actually level Jim. He fell back on the concrete floor on his own accord.

"Hogan knew something was wrong," he continued. "He came over to me and I said, 'Terry' (Hogan's given name was Terry Bollea), I'm done."

Hogan quickly got back in the ring and rolled Brutus Beefcake into a three-count pin for the decision.

Hogan and the referee quickly carried Jim back to the dressing area as the crowd screamed for Hulk Hogan and Hillbilly Jim, not knowing the severity of Jim's injury. This real life accident was not part of the show, and soon Jim was loaded into an ambulance taking him from the San Diego Sports Arena to the nearby Sharpe Cabrillo Hospital.

Jim caught a flash of luck upon learning that a noted orthopedic sports doctor, Tom Harris, who also worked with the U.S. Olympic Ski Team, had an office close to the hospital. That night Jim underwent emergency surgery.

"His kneecap, or patella, was completely dislodged by the kick," Harris said shortly after the surgery. "Technically, the impact of the blow ruptured what is called the patellar tendon, which helps hold the kneecap in place. As a result of this injury Jim was unable to straighten his leg at all."

Dr. Harris, an authority on sports medicine, and a doctor for several collegiate athletic teams and running clubs, had never seen such a devastating injury from a single blow.

"He said it was like being in a car wreck," Jim offered. "And for sure it was not something I needed at that time in my life."

The injury could have meant a quick end to one of the most promising careers in the WWF. Hillbilly Jim was on the verge of becoming a superstar.

"Because he was in such excellent physical condition, his recovery and rehabilitation progressed very well," Dr. Harris added. "Perhaps the most important element of Jim's condition is his flexibility, the ability of the joints to move fully. It helps prevent injuries and also, in case of damage, aids rehabilitation."

The surgeon continued:

"Tight muscles curb flexibility, while muscles that are in shape and stretch aid it. Trying to participate in a sport such as professional wrestling with muscles that are tight is like driving a car with the emergency brake on. When you try to stretch a tight muscle, the body reacts as if it were putting on the brakes."

Flexible hamstrings were the key to Jim's recovery, according to Dr. Harris.

"Once we reconnected his kneecap it was easier to teach his muscles to work at extending the knee again rather than if the hamstring muscle were tight."

Jim's blow to the knee was classified medically as direct trauma—sudden physical damage. There was no way to anticipate such a blow from Johnny Valiant's kick. No matter how well-conditioned, an athlete at any level is always vulnerable to direct trauma.

"When we first examined Jim, we were surprised and pleased that he realized the need for incredible conditioning," said Dr. Harris. "Jim and other professional wrestlers like him provide dramatic evidence that if you stretch and condition your body it has a much greater chance of escaping injury, and even if injury does occur, the odds of recovery are much brighter."

As Jim was loaded into the ambulance he wasn't sure what he was thinking.

At the time of the injury, Valiant offered that the kick was accidental. There was an element who thought his kick was no accident at all, but deliberate, an effort to put Hillbilly Jim out of wrestling.

The "accident" happened so fast and was so spontaneous that it was difficult to believe Valiant set out to maim Jim. However, it is easy to believe that once one of the WWF's most popular stars had been injured, McMahan's wrestling machine would turn it into another "good-versus-bad" script.

While adoring fans heaped flowers and cards on the wrestler from Mudlick, Kentucky, and other wrestlers called expressing a quick recovery, Luscious Johnny Valiant and Brutus Beefcake openly bragged they had "put the dumb Hillbilly in the hospital."

The fun-poking may have all been a part of the show in order to keep fan reaction at a fever pitch, and WWF publications did their part in keeping it alive that Hillbilly Jim just might have a score to settle if he ever wrestled again.

Jim Morris learned early in his wrestling career that it wasn't a matter *if* you were going to get hurt—it was when and how bad.

Chapter Two

Two weeks later Jim was on a plane with a full leg cast, from the bottom of his hip to the top of his ankle on his right leg.

Meeting him at the Nashville airport was good friend Bob Sanborn, who drove him back to his home town of Bowling Green where he immediately checked into Greenview Hospital.

"I stayed there for a couple of days just to make sure my knee was as it should be after the long flight," Jim said. "I was in the cast for nine weeks."

Jim and the WWF powers-to-be decided it would be best to return to San Diego to begin his rehabilitation. For some three weeks Jim stayed in the Radisson Suites Hotel while laboring through a strenuous program designed to get the wrestler back to where he would walk again.

"I wasn't sure at this point if I'd ever be able to walk normally again, much less compete against some of the best athletes in the world," he said.

Jim again returned to Bowling Green still rehabbing, and then back to San Diego to have several wires extracted that had been used to hold his injured knee in place.

The WWF and Vince McMahon had a sizable investment in Jim Morris. Engulfed in a whiz-bang marketing machine, they had morphed him into a stable of fine-tuned, pumped and chiseled gigantic athletes who pummeled, kicked, and blasted each other in a scripted show that even Hollywood envied. And thousands across the United States and throughout the world wanted to buy a ticket and see it.,

The fans couldn't get enough of the Hillbilly. Even when he wasn't in the ring they flocked to him…to get an autograph, to shake his hand, or just to hear his down-home-Kentucky drawl.

"I was voted the second most popular wrestler in the WWF, behind Hulk Hogan," Jim said. "And working with Hogan I was on track for $400,000 to $500,000 in 1985 when I got hurt. It probably cost me $750,000 to $800,000 over the next two years."

The WWF was not about to leave the big Kentuckian on the shelf. They knew his value, even when not in the ring.

The Hillbilly theme had worked so well that McMahan's agent, Joe Scarpa, a New Jersey Italian who had wrestled under the name of Chief Jay Strongbow, because of his resemblance to an American Indian, asked Jim if he knew of anyone who might be able to wrestle a little bit and carry on the hillbilly schtick.

"They had invested a lot of money in my character, so I told them about a wrestler I knew over in Jamestown, Kentucky, in Russell County," says Jim. "I had known Lanny Kean for a while and he became Cousin Junior. He was about 6'3", 255 lbs., and Vince and the guys really liked him."

Cousin Junior was an immediate hit, and it was only fitting that his first WWF match was in the Cow Palace in San Francisco. In his overalls he looked like the real deal, because he was. In an effortless sort of way he would drop into a semi-handstand propelling both legs behind him that usually landed in the face or chest of his opponent. When Cousin Junior delivered his "mule kick," it was match over.

With Hillbilly Jim continuing his rehab and now managing Cousin Junior, he was as visible as ever.

"Everybody loved him," Jim said. "The success, money, popularity and fringe benefits were just too much for him to handle. Finally, they (WWF) had had enough and sent him home."

In the meantime, Stan Frazier, a silo-sized Mississippian at 7-ft. 400 lbs., had been identified as a possible member of Jim's hillbilly family. Associated with legendary star-powered wrestling promoter Jimmy Hart, Frazier had played several characters over several years while entertaining mostly in the South.

"He became Uncle Elmer and the WWF brought Lanny (Cousin Junior) back and I was their manager," said Jim. "The crowd went crazy. We'd jump around and dance in the ring…having a good time even if we lost."

The "family" didn't lose much. The WWF was well aware of this wave and they were prepared to ride it for quite awhile. But, unfortunately, success doesn't always breed success; not all professional athletes are equipped mentally or socially to handle the rigors and fast-paced lifestyle of professional wrestling. Perhaps no other sport is more demanding night after night after night.

Once again, one of Jim's "family" members decided to swim against the current.

"I was with the WWF's A-team in Sacramento, California working with Hulk Hogan when Chief Strongbow, our agent, told me they were having a problem with Uncle Elmer," Jim said. "He was in Providence, Rhode Island doing an NBC network show against King Kong Bundy. Chief said Elmer refused to wrestle unless they agreed to pay him more money, and that I had to fly to Providence to take his place."

The WWF hustled up a Lear Jet, and soon Jim was headed once again cross country.

"It was an 18-passenger plane and I was the only one on it," he recalled. "The captain came back and said, 'you must be a very important person because this flight cost $18,000.'" Remember, this was in the '80s.

Knowing there would be little time between landing and climbing into the ring, Jim dressed into his wrestling gear on the plane. A limousine pulled up on the tarmac next to the jet once it stopped, and Jim climbed in, believing he was on his way to the Civic Center. But instead, the driver informed Jim there had been a sudden change in plans. Instead, he'd be going to a hotel.

At the last minute, Uncle Elmer showed up for his match.

"Vince had King Kong Bundy to beat him in 30 seconds, and when it was over they fired Uncle Elmer," Jim added.

"I was not happy with it at all. They gave me all of Elmer's shows instead of traveling with Hogan."

Still going with the family thing, Gene Lewis, a wrestler out of New Jersey, came on as Cousin Luke, and with Hillbilly Jim as Cousin Junior and Cousin Luke's manager, they defeated Greg "The Hammer" Valentine and Brutus Beefcake for the tag team title.

"Those guys got the break of a lifetime, but had problems with it all," Jim said. "You know, if it wasn't for my injury, that was the only reason they were brought in."

As Jim's knee began to heal and his tremendous conditioning began to pay off, the "family" began to break up for good. The WWF fazed out their bookings, and Hillbilly Jim was out to prove once again, "Don't go messin' with a country boy."

Chapter Three

*O*pal Houchens, Jim's mother, never had an easy life. Growing up in Barren County in the Lamb community in the late '40s, she married Goldman Brown, primarily to get away from home. The marriage, lacking a foundation of love, didn't last long, and soon she was on her own, a position she would come to know well for much of her life.

On March 21, 1953, Opal and William E. Morris were married in Springfield, Tennessee. But that marriage also didn't last long, with a divorce being granted in Allen County Circuit Court five months later.

Judge John B. Rodes granted her care and custody of son James Henry Morris with reasonable and proper rights of visitation with notice and reasonable time and place.

"I saw my dad twice in my life," Jim says. "I remember mama, my brother Dwight, and I drove out to his house in Scottsville to get some money. We had a wreck on the way home. My head went through the windshield and mama broke her nose. We had to run up the road to a house to get help. I was nine and Dwight six. They took us to Allen County War Memorial Hospital and put us all in the same room."

It was the same hospital where Jim was born in 1953. Weighing 5 lbs., 9-ounces and 19-inches in length, there was nothing to indicate his size would open the door to his future.

Jim, still reflecting on his early childhood:

"When I was little I never felt safe. I was a scared little kid, often having to go out into a dark, dark night and walk to a neighbor's house to use their phone to call a doctor for mama.

"We never had a back-up. I had no father or big brother, and a childhood that I thought could go off track at anytime."

Opal and her boys seemed to be in constant transition when it came to houses. There were a couple of moves while living in Glasgow where Jim attended E.B. Terry Elementary School. By 1964, the family had moved to nearby Scottsville in Allen County. Jim was 10-years-old.

Opal had found comfort and support in her church and her music, and she made her best effort to expose her two boys to both.

Opal attended the Church of God, with Pentecostal leanings, and James Henry and Dwight were always in tow. Soon Jim's personality began to emerge and before long he joined the rest of the congregation in song and shouting praises to God.

"Mama would drag me to church and to all of the tent meetings in our area," recalls Jim. "I was 10-years-old, and they would encourage me to testify. The crowds loved it when I got up in front of them. I knew how to whip 'em up, and I enjoyed it, too."

Albert Johnson had been a friend of Opal Morris' for several years. Moving to Evansville, Indiana to find work, he still stayed in contact with her through letters, returning periodically to visit with her and the boys, once even to help her move to a different house.

Opal and Albert shared their interest in the church and love of music, and his letters constantly warned her of the "evils of the world," and to avoid those who were trying to take advantage of her.

Jim's charisma and his ability to stand up and speak in front of others at such an early age was well received in the church by most, but not all.

Albert Johnson was quick to notice this, and in a letter to Opal referred to her son James as "God's little preacher," and then added, "people better leave him alone."

Jim liked Albert, he liked it that he and his mother were really into music, often writing gospel songs together. He also never forgot some advice he received from him.

"He said to me once, 'James Henry don't learn too much too quick… slow it down some'. I didn't really know what he was talking about back then. As I got older and going through life, it began to make sense."

The admiration Jim had for his mother never ceased. Recalling how she would stretch the $25 monthly welfare check plus what she got from Jim's dad—a check she had to go to court for—he grew to resent the lack of his dad's presence in his life.

"I had heard he lived in Indianapolis," Jim said. "And as soon as I turned 18 the money stopped. Never a Christmas card, never anything. He tried to come around when I started playing ball at Bowling Green High School, and then again when I started wrestling. Even then he'd try to go through someone else to contact me. I was never close to anyone on his side of the family, and it is hard to make up for 60 years."

For sure there wasn't money for the little extras in life for the Morris family. Opal's concern was food, housing and clothing. But there came a time in 1959 she went to Tommy Faught Furniture Company in Glasgow and splurged on a new Hotpoint Refrigerator that cost $229.44. Opal financed her purchase at New Farmers Bank of Glasgow, making $9.56 monthly payments over two years.

"People felt sorry for us," Jim recalled. "I hated that. Sorry is a sorry word and it weighed heavy on a little kid. I still hate people for the way my mother was treated. I can't help it. Our lot in life was bad. We were looked down on because of our financial situation."

Opal's family was worried about her, even to the point that one sister suggested she find someone to take Jim and Dwight for a while to relieve some of the pressure she was under. That stress was never more evident than when Opal physically attacked a welfare worker in 1967.

"It was a bad situation," Jim said years later. "She pushed mother to the limit. All of the stress of living like we were…finally the woman said the wrong thing."

The incident made the Bowling Green newspaper, and Police Judge George Boston probated any jail time for one year.

In a letter from her sisters, there was concern that Opal might have her boys taken away from her. But somehow, someway, she managed to hold it all together in some tough times, and still find a way to give to her church. She even received mailings from the J. Charles Jessup Radio Revival asking for a contribution.

Opal Morris, by this time, had gained a reputation as a pretty good guitar player, and her friend Albert Johnson was killer on the harmonica. "Good enough to play in Nashville," Jim says. She was insistent that Jim latch on to her passion for music. And to see that he had a good foundation, instead of buying him a bicycle when he was 10, she took him to Burkhart Music Store on Main Street in Bowling Green and purchased his first guitar.

"I think she paid $50 for it," says Jim. "I had learned to play one when I was eight. It was such a stretch for her to buy it, but it was so important for me to always have music in my life. She was so right in buying me a guitar instead of a bicycle. Its sort of like the 'teach a man to fish' saying. She made payments on it and later we traded it in on a Fender (guitar). It cost $126 and I still have it."

And what about that bicycle?

"Oh, I finally bought one myself when I was 18-years-old and out of high school. It was one of those with all those gears. I'm not sure half of them worked, but I finally had a bicycle to get around on."

Opal's vision for her oldest son may not have been obvious at the time, but perhaps it was her life experiences that gave her wisdom far beyond her years, and certainly her social status. Even without the trappings of high society, she always had her music to fall back on.

As Jim entered junior high in Scottsville, something else began to capture his interest other than church and music. It was basketball.

Almost a religion unto itself, there was good reason basketball at Allen County High School was literally on fire.

"When I went into junior high, Jim McDaniels was a senior," says Jim. "He was considered the best high school player in America. Everybody wanted to be Big Mac. And later, when I was a freshman at Bowling Green High, he was a freshman at Western Kentucky University. Basketball was all anybody talked about."

Unfortunately, many coaches didn't believe that sports and music could co-exist, so Jim Morris let his music slide as he began to fantasize that he could actually become a good basketball player despite being a skinny little kid.

In 1968, once again the Morris family was in transition, this time moving from Scottsville to Bowling Green where Jim finished his eighth grade year at Delafield School.

"Mama had had a few factory jobs over the years in Glasgow and Scottsville, but her biggest concern was Dwight and me. It would cost more to find someone to take care of us than she could make working," Jim said. "She wanted to leave Scottsville. Dwight was always into something, and she thought moving to Bowling Green would be a step up and a fresh start. Looking back, I'm not sure how my life would have worked out if we hadn't moved to Bowling Green. Back then there just seemed to be opportunities for us."

Opal and her boys settled into a concrete block building on Boatlanding Road, just a stone's throw from the Barren River.

"Remember, there were no food stamps back then," says Jim. "I just don't know how we did it with what we had. My mama was sick a lot, but if she'd been healthy she would have been a hellcat. She'd cuss and then she'd pray."

Although Jim might have pulled back a little on his music, Opal didn't on hers. She played guitar with Otis Blanton and the Blue Star Ranger Band, a local group that was in high demand throughout South Central Kentucky, and regularly played on the local Channel 13 television station in Bowling Green.

"The station was out on Morgantown Road, and Dwight and I would be right there watching and listening," says Jim. "She could play Wildwood Flower as good as Mother Maybelle Carter could."

From Boatlanding Road the family moved to Church Street. Opal was always looking to better her life and those of her two boys. She was a loving mother in spite of life not being easy.

Once again the decision was made to move. This time it was into one of the apartments in a subsidized housing complex called Bryant Village. With all of the moves in a brief time span, Jim and Dwight, who was named after President Dwight Eisenhower, were able to stay in the same school.

"Delafield was a nice school," Jim said. "Though it was mostly poor kids who went to school there."

He may not have had much money, and even though his school work didn't always show it, one thing Jim was not short of was brains. He was also a quick wit and savvy to the ways of the street.

Growing up in Bowling Green on the so-called wrong side of the tracks, his world was much different from many of his classmates who lived in more affluent neighborhoods.

"There were two schools on my side of town," he said. "The black kids went to Parker-Bennett School and Delefield, where I went. Us white kids that went to school there were considered poor white trash and rednecks. But I got along with everybody because I had started playing basketball."

Jim had seen what playing basketball could do to elevate a young boy's status when he lived in Scottsville, and now in a lesser way he was experiencing it himself by being a high school athlete.

"For the first time in my life I began to feel safe after we moved to Bowling Green and I began playing basketball," he says. "It gave me an identity and people began to admire me. I was more secure. I learned early that I could out talk the bullies in my neighborhood. I could read them and told them what they wanted to hear.

"When I did anything—basketball or music—I had to be good at it. I became driven," he said. "Much of it came from being told I could never do anything because of our economic situation. I knew I was going to have to do it on my own because I had no father, older brothers or uncles to help me."

The neighborhood the Morris family lived in was not without its street toughs and fights, but especially on weekends crime was fairly common.

"When we lived in Bryant Village it seemed like there was a shooting or stabbing every weekend," he continued. "The older kids called me four-eyes because of my glasses. But I always had a gift to gab so I'd talk to them and get to know the neighborhood toughs. Then I began to grow and build myself up and they didn't want to mess with me. I got bigger, stronger, and more impressive looking, and some of the bullies didn't want to take a chance with me. Unfortunately, it was the little guys who had to fight more."

Living in the area where Jim did often meant you didn't have to go looking for trouble to find it…it could find you. He was walking home from basketball practice his freshman year, and with his tied Converse basketball shoes slung over his shoulder and a small gym bag in one hand, he walked past Wiley's Bar on lower Main Street.

"The door was open, so being a kid I just looked in the door," he remembers. "It was dark, but I heard a guy yell at me, 'What'd you say?' I just kept walking, and he came out and asked me what I had said. He was drunk. I told him I didn't say anything and kept walking. All of a sudden I felt a pain in my lower back and reached around and felt blood. He had cut me. I turned around and shoved him down and kicked him several times."

Fortunately someone by then had called the police, who in turn took Jim to the City-County Hospital where it took 15 stitches to close the cut.

"The police took me home," he said. "Mama was really worried, wondering why I hadn't already gotten home. I couldn't call her because we didn't have a phone. In fact, we didn't have a phone until I went away to college in Oklahoma and saved enough money for us to have one. I remember if we had an important call to make we'd go next door and use their phone. Every time we did it, they'd always say, 'don't make a long distance call.'"

Chapter Four

*B*asketball, basketball and more basketball; that's all Jim Morris thought about. The memories of Coach Jimmy Bazzell's great Allen County teams stuck with him, and even though he was now living in Bowling Green and doing everything he could to be good enough to become a Bowling Green High School Purple, his new found friends and teammates still referred to him as "Allen County." It's a name that has stuck with him over a lifetime from his high school basketball teammates, although some shortened it to "County."

The nickname was one Jim Morris could live with. After all, Allen County (Scottsville) High School was one of the premier basketball programs in all of Kentucky. Coach Jimmy Bazzell, in 17 years rang up 404 wins with only 91 losses. That's an 82% winning percentage. During that same time span Bowling Green High was 213-242 with nine different coaches, so calling Jim "Allen County" was done with a degree of respect because of where he had come from. Basketball was big, and Bowling Green desired the success of their neighboring county.

When basketball Coach Larry Doughty prepared for the 1968-69 season at Bowling Green High after coming off a 13-15 season, he felt a bit of relief in knowing he had a handful of returning players that included a solid B-team.

The future looked bright.

Doughty and his Purples rebounded the following season with a 25-5 record that included a 76-75 win in the 14th District finals over host Franklin-Simpson. In the regional semi-finals however, Bowling Green fell to Auburn 81-79 while Franklin Simpson, on the verge of becoming Bowling Green's biggest rival, beat Auburn in the finals to advance to the Sweet 16.

The 1969-70 season would turn out to be the last for Doughty. Although he had played some basketball at Western Kentucky University, mostly as a reserve, he was always considered a "baseball man." He starred in that sport for the Hilltoppers, and it was a dream come true when he departed the prep coaching ranks to join the Cincinnati Red's baseball organization as a full time scout.

His 24-4 record was evident that the Purples had turned the corner, even though they fell to Allen County 68-67 in the Regional finals.

Some thought Doughty was getting out while the gettin' was good. After all, he would be leaving the new coach with only one returning starter. The Purples All-State Mike Larson had signed with Western, and only guard Frank Ragland would be back.

Don Webb had been Doughty's assistant for two years. He knew the program, but most of all he knew what was in the basketball pipeline at Bowling Green. Before the term became popular, Webb was "a player's coach." They loved and respected him. It was common knowledge to those at the high school that he was not just about basketball.

Though Webb had a few detractors when his name came up to follow Doughty, he had the support of principal Chet Redmon, and Superintendent W.R. McNeill. But, in an almost unprecedented move of support, some 30 students showed up before the school board in praise of Coach Webb. They spoke how he related to students on and off the basketball court, and how he gave students an incentive to make good grades and graduate.

Soon after, the 38-year-old Webb was named the thirteenth head coach since the program began in 1922.

Webb knew he had some talent. Even though the varsity team the year before had gone 24-4, his B-team had beaten them twice in head-to-head competition.

Webb held his cards close to his chest, knowing the cupboard was far from bare.

"I moved the junior varsity right into the starting lineup with Ragland," Webb said. "Those guys could play and now it was their turn to prove it."

Webb felt good knowing he had a nucleus of Frank Ragland, Steve Carter and Jim Morris that just might be one of the best Purple squads of all-time.

These three along with Tommy Duncan, Lloyd Campbell, Kevin Redman, Phil Cooke, David Mullendore, and sophomore Martin Reubin, carried the load for Webb during his first season as head coach.

Webb had brought in as his assistant coach a kid right out of college by the name of Stan Markham. He was well known in the Bowling Green and Western communities as a baseball player, and for good reason. In 1965 he pitched Bowling Green High to a state baseball title winning all three games. The left-hander followed his high school coach, Jim Pickens, to Western with aspirations of some day reaching the bigs. It was not to be, however, as an arm injury on a cold spring night while pitching in Class A ball in South Dakota ended it all.

"I came back home, got my degree, and jumped at the chance to be Don Webb's assistant at Bowling Green," he said. "I had played four years of basketball in high school for four different coaches, so I did have some varied knowledge of the game."

It didn't take the two new coaches long, with virtually an all new team, to realize they just might have something special.

By now Frank Ragland had become a coach on the floor, and in Stan Markham's words, "The best little point guard around…a coach on the floor." Steve Carter was a lights out shooter, who early on in his senior year was drawing attention from several Division I teams. But it was Jim Morris who had locked in on his game, now realizing that he might have a future in basketball, perhaps maybe, just maybe going to college. For Jim, even reaching his senior year of high school was an accomplishment, and no one was more proud than his mother, Opal. It might even be an incentive for younger brother Dwight to follow suit.

With a not so easy home life, Jim had already overcome situations that would have caused others to dropout and become nothing more than a statistic. Coach Webb had made it clear that if he wanted to play basketball, he had to attend class and make passing grades.

"Coach Webb understood my home situation. When you have nothing in life and all you have to hang onto is basketball…that's what I was hanging onto," Jim offered. "One time he took me to Sears and got me some clothes; I was growing so fast, I didn't have many. I think he got me some pants, shirts, a sweater, jacket and it seems like some shoes and an overcoat for winter. I needed some new glasses, too, and he got me some through a Lions Club program."

Throughout the year his glasses would be held together with pieces of tape, and lots of time he wore an elastic strap attached to them even when not playing basketball.

"He didn't want to play any other sports or go to class," Don Webb recalled. "It was just basketball."

For the time being there was really not a place for Jim's music, now that he was playing basketball.

"Back then there was a stupid mindset that if you played sports you couldn't play music," he said.

By now Jim was a bit over 6-5 and his weight was 205 lbs.. Although his appearance was still a slight build, and wearing horned-rimmed glasses, he could have been called Clark Kent instead of "Allen County." It was amazing that at no time was he ever talked to about playing football. "I was just a skinny white kid," he laughed.

If it wasn't bad enough that there was never an effort to get Jim on the football field think about this. In his senior year Bowling Green High had begun a wrestling program. That's right, a wrestling program. And like football, Jim Morris was not on its roster.

"I do remember when they started wrestling," he said. "But I didn't really want to do that either. I was afraid I'd get hurt."

His game had taken on a Superman-like status, and no longer was he being pushed around on the basketball court or more importantly in his neighborhood.

Between Jim's junior and senior year of high school he was befriended by a young man four years his elder. The friendship became life changing in that the two of them began a regiment of weight training and a special diet.

Tommy Hagan had gone to St. Joseph Catholic School located in the same area of town where Jim lived.

"Tommy was a brick layer and we became best buddies," Jim said. "He'd take his money and buy weights at Herman Lowe Sporting Goods down on State Street. We'd buy eggs, steaks, milk and anything else we thought would help make us bigger and stronger."

For Jim's part, he wasn't exactly rolling in extra money to support his "training table" diet, so there might have been occasions when a few steaks found their way to Jim's bicycle as he peddled away from one of the local downtown grocery stores.

Hagan lived on Scott Street, not all that far from Jim, which made it an easy bicycle ride to get back and forth for their weight lifting session in the backyard at Tommy's house.

"We made a bench out of scrap lumber," Hagan said years later. "It seemed like all we did was lift weights and play basketball. We played all over town on any outdoor courts or gyms we could sneak into."

Hagan continues:

"Our families didn't have much so we'd mow yards to eat. I remember all those 50-cent Yum Burgers we used to eat at the Burger Basket."

Hagan, being a few years older than Jim, offered that their close friendship drew several critical comments from several people around Bowling Green.

"The word was out that I'd get Jim drunk during his senior year of high school," Hagan says. "So I went to Coach Webb to get everything cleared up. He was okay with Jim and I, even letting me go to away games with them.

"There might have been times over the years Jim and I drank a little vodka, but not to get drunk…just to relax," he added. "We really liked putting the hustle on a few of the college guys back then. We'd take a couple of empty vodka bottles, wash them out and fill them up with water. Then we'd go to one of the basketball courts where they were and act like we were drinking vodka straight out of the bottle. Of course it was only water, but they didn't know it. We'd stagger around shooting baskets. Then they'd want to play us for money. We wore 'em out."

Hagan transferred to Bowling Green High after his sophomore year at St. Joseph when the high school was closed down.

"I was a pretty good basketball player back then, even though I was only 5-8, but if you weren't black or a white boy with influence it was difficult to make the team. That's just the way it was."

Black or white, Jim Morris and Tommy Hagan got along with everyone, even to the point that Hagan says he, Jim, and Dwight were the only white boys welcome in the neighborhood.

"We had each others back," says Hagan.

Hagan graduated from Bowling Green High in 1968, and more than a decade later entered Western where he got his teaching degree. For some 25 years he has been teaching in Nashville, Tennessee.

In the meantime, basketball had become an obsession for Jim. He idolized Jim McDaniels, the 7-foot All-American at Western who he first saw play at Allen County.

"I even wore his #44 my senior year at Bowling Green High. I couldn't get enough of basketball…played it every day of my life back then. It didn't matter if there was snow on the ground or not, and most of the time the goals didn't have nets. I didn't care. Frank Ragland and I would go to the old high school gym on Center Street and play even when it was closed. Frank had a window he could slip through and we'd get in.

"It was tough living in Bryant Village. There was a stabbing or shooting every weekend," says Jim. "I just did my best to get along with everybody and the fact that I had become a pretty good basketball player earned some respect in the neighborhood."

While most of Jim's white teammates had cars, or at least access to one on weekends, his preferred mode of transportation was a bicycle or walking. Owning a car or being able to drive his mother's was out of the question. In fact, it wasn't a big deal for him. There were many times he would pedal over to the local Boys Club, just a few blocks from his house. It was here he found solace away from some of the older adults in his neighborhood.

Another youngster who grew up around the Boys Club was Stan England, who was a few years older than Jim.

"I grew up in the Delafield area," says England years later. "I was the toughest white boy on the basketball court back then. I went up to Flint, Michigan for a while to play some ball."

When England returned to Bowling Green, he was in for a surprise.

"I went down to the Boys Club and out on the court was this tall, muscular guy really turning it on. 'Who is that' I asked?"

England was told it was Jim Morris, who played ball here when he was little and was a star at Bowling Green High.

"Then it came to me," England said. "He was the little, scrawny kid I used to hold down so he couldn't get his shot off. I immediately went over to him and re-introduced myself to him and took him to lunch."

England later followed in the footsteps of Charlie Collins and ran the Boys Club for several years, often bringing Jim Morris back to talk to the kids about the things they could accomplish in life.

"He was a great spokesman," says England. "And he made himself available anytime I asked even though he was a big star."

"The Boys Club was the salvation of lots of kids who lived on my side of the tracks," Jim said. "The director, Mr. Charles Collins, made sure we had a safe place to hang out."

But Jim takes the influence Collins had on needy youngsters a step further.

"Mr. Collins would hire several of us to do some work around the club," Jim recalled. "I'll never forget when he paid us for the first time. He loaded us all in that van of his and took us to a bank in town, and made us open a savings account. I was probably a freshman in high school then, and he taught me something about money I never forgot.

"Some of my buddies would go back soon after and get all of their money out to spend. Heck, I kept money in my account and have never been without a bank account after Mr. Collins explained to me why I needed to do it."

Jim continues:

"I had seen my poor mother take a piece of paper and sit at the kitchen table and try to figure out how she was going to pay her bills. She'd pay $9 dollars here, $6 dollars there, and $8 dollars another place, just hoping to have enough to keep a roof over our head. I never wanted it to be that way for me."

Charles Collins, who with his close-cropped hair resembled Sgt. Carter from the Gomer Pyle Show, could be seen on a regular basis hauling his boys around Bowling Green, making sure they learned more than just hanging out.

"We had an old Ford Econoline Van at the high school," says Stan Markham, the former assistant coach. "We practiced at what was then the new gym, and I'd take Jim and all of our black players who lived in the same neighborhood home after practice."

Teammate, Steve Carter, also remembers dropping Jim off at Bryant Village.

"I'd take the guys home on occasion. It was a little scary where they lived. Back then it was a racist environment, but we all, regardless of our skin color, had great camaraderie as a team. "County," as we called him, just fit in with both groups. He was such a unique person even back then before the wrestling thing and all. We never talked about any of the social issues among our team. We were just teammates."

Lots of times it's the manager of the team who knows more of what's going on with the team than anyone else. The manager has the ears of the coaches and the players. He gets it from both sides. Jim Robinson, who later became Dr. Jim Robinson, a Bowling Green dentist, was that person at Bowling Green High.

"The coaches and players both trusted me," Dr. Jim says. "I had the keys to the gym and even oversaw an account to buy supplies that we needed for the team at one of the sporting goods stores."

While Coach Markham had used a school van to take the guys home, there were times when Robinson's 1961 white VW Beetle was the ride of the day.

"I had an 8-track player under the right front seat," he laughed. "I'd have Jim and me in the front, and either Lloyd Campbell, Frank Ragland or Ernie Harpool squeezed in the back. We had fun.

"I could tell there were times when I took Jim home that he really didn't want to go. I'd ask him if he was okay and he'd say, 'I'll be all right.'"

Robinson later, because of Don Webb's recommendation, got a student-athlete trainer scholarship to Western.

"I came back to Bowling Green from dental school in 1979 and saw Jim. He had bulked up from the skinny kid I used to know."

Lloyd Campbell was one of Jim's black teammates who lived in the same neighborhood. He was an eighth grader at St. Joe Catholic School when Jim moved in as a high school freshman. The two became close friends.

"We played ball all the time on the outdoor courts," Campbell says. "He was tall, real skinny, and a real character...always fun to be with."

Campbell, who became one of Bowling Green High School's best defensive players, never forgot Jim Morris's best trait of all.

"He was color blind during a period of racial strife in the late '60s and early '70s," he offered. "Back then that stood out. He came over to my house a lot, even after he went to college. My father was deceased and he'd visit my mother and sister."

Perhaps no one saw the future that Lloyd Campbell would have either with a 27-year career with the Department of Defense. But, neither did Lloyd see his friend Jim's career going into professional wrestling.

"No one saw it coming," he laughed. "But in thinking about it, it is just another one of 'Allen County's' characters...but he's anything but a hillbilly."

Chapter Five

*A*s Coach Don Webb readied his team for the 1970-71 season, with only one returning starter from the previous year's 24-4 squad, the uncertainties outweighed the certainty.

Webb had coached at Edmonson County and Richardsville before joining Larry Doughty's staff, and with only what was perceived as a good group of juniors with little varsity experience, the upcoming season was anybody's guess—except Webb's.

In the season opener, Bowling Green *Daily News* Sports Editor Bert Borrone described the team's win over Olmstead like this:

"Jim Morris tossed in a school-record 41 points as Bowling Green High opened its basketball season with a 105-49 romp past Olmstead here last night.

"The 6-5 center hit on 18 of 28 attempts from the field and cashed five of 10 free throws as Coach Don Webb's Purples showed far too much for the invaders.

"Morris also picked off 19 rebounds, one more than the entire opposing team.

"Also in double figures were Frank Ragland with 15 points and Steve Carter with 10."

Yes, Superman, although still wearing his glasses, had arrived on the scene. And along with him came an entourage of talent that would equally share the spotlight on the basketball court during a season that quickly now looked more certain than not.

If Jim Morris had anything to say about the team's future success, part of it would lay to rest a heartbreaking 68-67 Fourth Regional final loss to his namesake, Allen County the year before.

When the *Courier-Journal*'s first week's Litkenhous Ratings came out, there at the top was Bowling Green High.

"It was a bit premature," Don Webb said at the time. "We won our first two and then we were clobbered at home by Franklin-Simpson by 29 points, 87-58. Franklin was the only team to beat our junior varsity last year. The number one ranking made our kids tight. They weren't prepared for it."

And neither was Webb. He was prepared enough, however, to get his team settled down and back on track.

High school schedules are made in advance, but not to the degree of colleges, who set their schedule three or four years out. And although the Purple coaching staff that included Larry Doughty before his departure put together an ambitious schedule for the "inexperienced" Purples, there remained enough flexibility to add to it if the right opportunity came along.

Initially, there was a 23-game card that included several district and regional foes, plus the likes of Paducah Tilghman, Louisville Central, Daviess County, Earlington, Louisville Westport, Christian County, and Todd Central.

Suddenly, Bowling Green High was in demand. Scoring over 100 points in several games and averaging well over 90, Don Webb's team had become a scoring machine, thanks to Jim Morris, Steve Carter and Frank Ragland. The three of them were hitting at over 20-points each.

Basketball crazies across Kentucky really took notice when Bowling Green, ranked #6, defeated #3 Louisville Central, 73-67 the day after Christmas in 1970, on the big stage of Freedom Hall in a preliminary to the ABA Kentucky Colonels professional team.

Frank Ragland showed his stuff with 26 points, while Tommy Duncan added 20 and Steve Carter 15. The four points Jim scored were his lowest of the season, as he was often doubled teamed inside forcing the ball outside for open looks.

In the meantime, Don Webb had been invited to take his team to Nashville to be a part of a prep triple header at Vanderbilt's Memorial Gymnasium. Beating Tennessee's #4 ranked Clarksville High 78-73, #4 ranked Bowling Green could now set its sights on once again playing in Freedom Hall in Louisville.

For the first time in school history, Bowling Green received an invitation to the prestigious Louisville Invitational Tournament, which many consider a preview to the State Tournament. Louisville Atherton fell in the first round 54-50, as Jim Morris scored 17 points and grabbed 18 boards. Carter added 12.

The win set up a rematch with Louisville Central. The Yellowjackets put the sting on the Purples 89-74. Carter, however, put on a shooting display hitting 10 of 20 from the field, and 7 of 7 at the foul line for 27 points. Ragland's 17 and Morris 11 rounded out double figure scoring.

With an 18-2 record, Bowling Green, in mid-February, traveled to Louisville again and defeated #8 ranked Westport 90-75, Ragland's 28 and Carter's 23 led the way. Morris did his share with 15 points and 20 rebounds.

In the last regular season home game of the year, Jim had what many called his best effort of the season, with 21 points and 21 rebounds, in an 84-69 win over Hart County. Close behind were Ragland and Carter with 20 and 17 each.

The Purples had a fantastic regular season, losing only to Franklin-Simpson, Louisville Central, and in the last game at Todd Central 83-70. Heading into the district tourney with a 22-3 mark, a trip to the Sweet 16 looked very promising.

—⚏—

The 14th District tournament was played on the campus of Western Kentucky University in Diddle Arena, a 12,500-seat venue that had just experienced the play of one of Western's all-time great teams that actually reached the NCAA Final Four in the Houston Astrodome. Led by All-American Jim McDaniels, the Hilltoppers had been accustomed to playing to a full house in Diddle Arena. For the four high school teams playing on the same floor as some of those great Western teams was exciting, plus it would give them the opportunity of playing on a college size floor in a large arena atmosphere, much like they would experience should they reach the State Tournament, then being played in Louisville's Freedom Hall. It was a site the Purples were familiar with, having played three games there during the season.

In the opening game, Bowling Green disposed of Warren East, an up and coming powerhouse, by a 72-61 score. East was led by a pair of juniors, Johnny Britt and Charles Fishback. Britt would go on to become one of the all-time greats at Western, while Fishback had a stellar career at Austin Peay. (Fishback is also the father to Daymeon Fishback, a Kentucky Mr. Basketball in 1996 at Greenwood High School.)

Coach Frank Cardwell's Franklin Simpson squad defeated Warren Central 79-45 to reach the finals against Bowling Green. Remember: both winner and runner-up in District play qualify for the Regionals.

A Bowling Green-Franklin-Simpson final in anything meant a spirited crowd, and this game would not disappoint.

Eight thousand screaming fans showed up to see what Bowling Green *Daily News* columnist, Bert Borrone, called "the greatest comeback in the history of the 14th District," after the Purples streaked to a 31-11 second quarter lead before falling to Franklin 91-87.

The Wildcats Donnie Bland and James Griffin paced the winners with 25 and 17 points respectively.

Jim Morris led the way in a losing effort with 22 points on 10 of 12 from the field. But it was one shot he made that didn't count, and according to some launched Franklin-Simpson toward their comeback win.

No one there that night will ever forget what took place. With 5:28 left in the first half and Bowling Green on top 38-19, Jim gathered up a loose ball and headed toward his basket. For sure he was the only one in Diddle Arena who knew what was getting ready to happen.

As he approached the foul line he began to elevate, and when he came down he became the first high school player to dunk the basketball in an actual game in Diddle Arena. There was only one problem… it didn't count. At the time dunking was not allowed in high school or college, and if a player did it, it was a technical foul.

Jim Morris' dunk wasn't just a dunk, it was a two-handed thunder slam. But immediately the whistle blew among boos from the Franklin-Simpson fans and a spattering of cheers from the Purple side who mostly stood in silence, not knowing if it counted or not.

"I just had to do it," Jim said years later. "I thought it would fire us up. I knew it wouldn't count, but we had a big lead. I had seen Big Mac (Jim McDaniels) dunk a couple of weeks before against Murray and how crazy the crowd reacted. I wanted to do the same thing. I thought this would be the stamp (on the letter) to send them home."

But it didn't work out that way.

"All of a sudden I felt the air go out of my teammates," he recalled. "But I knew Coach Webb deep-down liked it. He had that little sheepish grin of his, but then he went back to his coaching mode."

Jim says the sequence was a defining moment for him as far as athletics were concerned.

"I thought my teammates quit on me after that. I was so into the game and at that very instant I realized team sports weren't for me," he said. "There may have been some jealousy, I'm not sure. I had done something they may have wanted to do."

Jim continued:

"I didn't do it for a look-at-me-moment. Franklin Simpson had killed us earlier in the year and I wanted to run them out of there and embarrass them like they had done to us. I was into the moment and thought it (the dunk) would get us fired up. Instead of motivating my team the air went out.

"We hated Franklin and they hated us. There wasn't any hand shaking and all of that silly stuff they do today."

Jim Morris never dreamed his team would lose that game, and years later, reflecting on it, he knows his dunk didn't cost his team the win.

"Hell, I knew the score. It was the district and we were already in the regionals," he said. "So we had a safety net. Earlier I had a couple of chances to dunk on lob passes from Tommy Duncan. Basketball was all I had then, but that changed my feeling for team sports. With my weight lifting, it was me and the weight. As for wrestling, it was me, and me alone with my opponent… no one else to blame if I failed."

Assistant Stan Markham remembers it well.

"You could see it in his eyes as he headed for the goal," he said. "And when he did it, our reaction on the bench was 'what have you done'? I heard Frank Cardwell, their coach, yelling at his players, 'Are you going to let him make a fool out of you?'"

Teammate Lloyd Campbell will never forget it either.

"I was getting ready to check in the game," he says. "I couldn't believe he did it. It didn't seem real. It definitely inspired Franklin Simpson."

Jim's dunk was on the order of something you would see in an NBA Slam dunk contest. He was that much of a leaper. In high school, on a barometer "jumping apparatus" in Diddle Arena, he once measured 11 feet 10 inches, nearly two feet above the rim.

"You know how hyenas hate lions and lions hate hyenas?" Jim asked. "That's how we were between our teams back then."

Franklin-Simpson coach Frank Cardwell agreed.

"For the fans it was a bitter rivalry," he said. "But Don (Webb), Stan (Markham) and I got along great."

Cardwell remembered the dunk well, too.

"Jim got a runout and about tore the goal down. People don't really know how good of a basketball player he was. He could dominate a game. We hit the technical foul shot, got the ball out and scored. We then started pressing all over the floor and turned it around. Tony Atkins had four straight steals that turned into baskets."

With Franklin and Bowling Green both advancing to the 4th Regional Tournament, also played in Diddle Arena, anything other than a rematch in the finals would be an upset.

Bowling Green did its part, defeating Tompkinsville and Adairville. Against Tompkinsville Jim scored 29 and hauled in 11 rebounds. In the Adairville game he rang up 38 points and 14 boards. Franklin-Simpson narrowly escaped with a 66-65 win over Glasgow, before beating Metcalfe County to set up a showdown with the Purples for a trip to the Sweet 16.

It did not disappoint!

The 9,000 fans saw the Purples jump out to an early 11-2 lead, before Franklin-Simpson caught fire and trailed only 40-38 at the half.

With just over two minutes left in the third quarter and Bowling Green on top 58-50 a foul called against the Purples brought a showering of paper cups onto the Diddle Arena floor. Immediately a technical foul was whistled against the Bowling Green crowd as Coach Webb raced to the P.A. to appeal to the crowd.

Once again a technical had turned the tide in two straight games with the two rivals.

The Wildcats hit the foul shot and then a field goal to cut the lead to five. The momentum had shifted.

It came down to less than 10 seconds in the game. After a Purple turnover, Franklin's James Griffin put up a 22-footer that fell short, only to be grabbed by teammate Donnie Bland, who put it in the basket from five feet out with one-second on the clock for a 79-77 win.

Years later Bland recalled something long overlooked.

"The reason James' shot was short was because big Jim Morris jumped and got a block on it. That's why it was short and I happened to be in the right spot to get it."

Bland, reflecting back on the rivalry with Bowling Green, recalls that when his team beat the number one ranked Purples early in the season by 29 it knocked them out of a feature the Louisville *Courier-Journal* was going to write.

"Instead they did it on us," he says. "We were the only Franklin-Simpson team to ever beat Bowling Green three times in the same year, all in Bowling Green. You know, in my career, there were only a handful of guys I played against who I felt were my equal or maybe even a little better, and Jim Morris was one of them."

That quick it was over for Jim and his teammates. He had scored 24 points to go with nine rebounds, and along with Frank Ragland and Steve Carter was named to the All-Tournament team. For the three games, the kid they called "Allen County" had averaged just over 30 points and 11 rebounds a game.

"That team had as much talent as any team I ever had," says Webb, who tallied 99 wins and 35 losses in his five years as a head coach that included a trip to the Sweet 16 in 1973. "Jim was such a huge part of it all, and the fact that he never played football allowed him to really be dedicated to the game. His work ethic and excitement made me think he could definitely play in college."

Chapter Six

*C*ollege was something Jim had not spent a great amount of time thinking about. Dealing with high school was tough enough. But suddenly he was receiving letters from college coaches interested in recruiting him to play basketball.

Some of the schools, however, were leery of Jim's grades. Readily admitting he did not like classroom work, he nevertheless knew he had to do it. Falling behind on the needed credits for a high school diploma when it came time to graduate, Jim was left out.

"In my mind teachers were sometime glorified babysitters," Jim said. "I could not get motivated in a classroom. I love to read and absorb everything I read."

Billy Madison had been a guidance counselor at Bowling Green High for several years, and he, like everyone else at the school wanted to see the youngster get his diploma. He saw how dedicated Jim was on the basketball court, and after several conversations, Madison persuaded Jim he needed to apply the same effort in order to graduate.

"Jim was always well-mannered and so appreciative of efforts on his behalf," Madison recalled. "He needed an English and math class, and the only way he could do it was summer school." "I told him if he came to summer school and made the effort I'd see that he graduated. He was one of those kids who responded when encouraged. And he made the effort."

What happened next was something that Billy Madison, Coach Don Webb and Jim Morris never forgot.

"It was in August, and Billy and I drove down to Jim's house on Gordon Avenue to give him his diploma," Webb says. "It was very emotional. We handed it to him and we all cried."

Forgotten were the heartbreaking losses in the District and Regional finals to Franklin-Simpson. Forgotten was Jim's dunk in Diddle Arena that resulted in that technical foul. Forgotten, too, were the missed class assignments. What mattered now was that Jim had achieved something much more difficult than his all-tournament and all-state recognition. He was now officially a Bowling Green High School graduate.

He was proud, but not nearly as proud as his mother, Opal. Perhaps she thought now her son just might go to college after all.

One of those colleges was Western Kentucky University, where the Hilltoppers had just completed the greatest season in the school's history, reaching the NCAA Final Four in Houston.

"We looked at Jim but had signed Mike Larson, a 6-5 player from Bowling Green High the year before," said Jim Richards, who at the time was an assistant at Western under John Oldham. "We weren't sure about his grades then, and looking back on it maybe we should have looked at him a little closer. He was such a natural talent, and who knew how much bigger he would get."

In early October 1970, Jim received a letter from the University of North Carolina at Charlotte head coach Bill Foster, along with a "no-postage-necessary" inquiry card. (Foster later coached at Duke in the mid-to-late 1970s.) Jim, 16-years-old, filled it out, signed it, but never mailed it back.

"Mom and I decided I didn't want to go to school that far away," Jim says. "And besides, the school wasn't well known back then."

On April 18, 1971, Jim and his mother, in green ink, signed a grant-in-aid scholarship letter to attend Cumberland College of Tennessee Junior College in Lebanon, Tennessee. Head Coach and Director of Athletics Russ Day had also signed it, stipulating that Jim would have a full scholarship commitment for one school year beginning September 12, 1971.

Less than a month later, Jim received another letter from Cumberland College and Coach Day informing Jim that Day was no longer the coach at the Junior College.

"I do not know where I am going to be coaching next year," he wrote. "I will be glad to have you wherever I go."

Day encouraged Jim not to pass up any good scholarship offers and added, "The main thing for you to do right now is to graduate."

For whatever reason, Jim and his mother had not yet returned the signed scholarship paper to Cumberland College, so he was still free to choose a college.

Opal, 1944

Opal with Cousin Thelma in 1944

Opal   James Henry (baby photo)

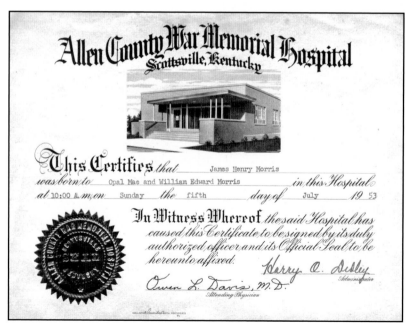

Birth certificate showing Jim's weight and length

James Henry, age 4, with Dwight, age 1

James Henry, age 6   *James Henry, age 7*

James Henry, age 10

E.B. Terry Elementary School in Glasgow where Jim went to school

James Henry, age 10, and Dwight, age 7, with Santa

James Henry, age 11, and Dwight, age 8

Dwight, age 9

Jim, 6th grade

Jim (pictured front row, glasses, white shoes), 7th grade in Scottsville, Ky.

Jim, Tommy Duncan and Lloyd Campbell were recognized in the Bowling Green High School student newspaper for their Purple Power on the basketball team in December 1970.

Freshman year, page 169 of the Bowling Green High School yearbook, 1968. Jim is #13.

This is the 1969-70 team in Jim's junior year.

The 1970-71 Purple team.

Jim's high school coaches: assistant coach Stan Markham and head coach Don Webb.

Ragland Hits 26

Purples Hand No. 3 Central 73-67 Loss

Male Still Tops

Purples Ranked 4th In State Prep Poll

Louisville Male On Bill

Purples' Cagers To Play In Hall Of Fame Tilt At Vandy

Face Central Saturday

Purples Have 91.6 Average On Season

Male Rated No. 1

BGH Ranked 6th In State In AP Prep Basketball Poll

An assortment of headlines during Jim's senior season

Purples Flash 11-1 Mark, 9 Straight Wins

Ragland Stars

Morris Has 38, BGH Tips Adairville 95-78

Purples Prevail 54-50

Morris, Carter Spark BGH To LIT Win Over Atherton

Purples Romp 105-49

BGH's Morris Gets Record 41 In Opener

Carter Scores 22

Purples Rout Caverna, For Sixth Win In Row

An assortment of headlines during Jim's senior season

58

ALL-TOURNAMENT TEAM — Front row (left to right): Johnny Britt, Warren East; Charles Fishback, Warren East; Frank Ragland, Bowling Green High; Jim Morris, Bowling Green High. Back row: Donnie Bland, Franklin-Simpson; Ricky Bell, Franklin-Simpson; David Beckner, Warren Central; James Griffin, Franklin-Simpson; Brad Grow, Franklin-Simpson; Greg McKinney, Warren Central.

All District team

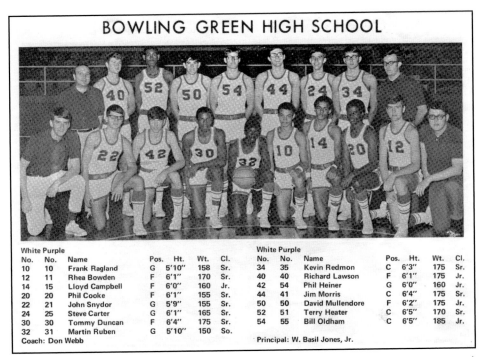

BOWLING GREEN HIGH SCHOOL

White	Purple	Name	Pos.	Ht.	Wt.	Cl.
No.	No.					
10	10	Frank Ragland	G	5'10''	158	Sr.
12	11	Rhea Bowden	F	6'1''	170	Sr.
14	15	Lloyd Campbell	F	6'0''	160	Jr.
20	20	Phil Cooke	F	6'1''	155	Sr.
22	21	John Snydor	G	5'9''	155	Sr.
24	25	Steve Carter	G	6'1''	165	Sr.
30	30	Tommy Duncan	F	6'4''	175	Sr.
32	31	Martin Ruben	G	5'10''	150	So.

Coach: Don Webb

White	Purple	Name	Pos.	Ht.	Wt.	Cl.
No.	No.					
34	35	Kevin Redmon	C	6'3''	175	Sr.
40	40	Richard Lawson	F	6'1''	175	Jr.
42	54	Phil Heiner	G	6'0''	160	Jr.
44	41	Jim Morris	C	6'4''	175	Sr.
50	50	David Mullendore	F	6'2''	175	Jr.
52	51	Terry Heater	C	6'5''	170	Sr.
54	55	Bill Oldham	C	6'5''	185	Jr.

Principal: W. Basil Jones, Jr.

Bowling Green played in the prestigious LIT in January of 1971. Here is the team. Note Jim's (#44) height and weight.

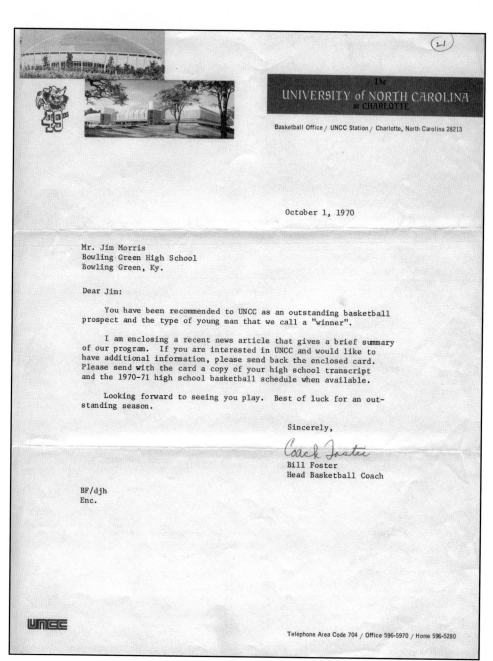

The
UNIVERSITY of NORTH CAROLINA
at CHARLOTTE

Basketball Office / UNCC Station / Charlotte, North Carolina 28213

October 1, 1970

Mr. Jim Morris
Bowling Green High School
Bowling Green, Ky.

Dear Jim:

You have been recommended to UNCC as an outstanding basketball prospect and the type of young man that we call a "winner".

I am enclosing a recent news article that gives a brief summary of our program. If you are interested in UNCC and would like to have additional information, please send back the enclosed card. Please send with the card a copy of your high school transcript and the 1970-71 high school basketball schedule when available.

Looking forward to seeing you play. Best of luck for an outstanding season.

Sincerely,

Coach Foster

Bill Foster
Head Basketball Coach

BF/djh
Enc.

Telephone Area Code 704 / Office 596-5970 / Home 596-5280

Letter from Coach Bill Foster at UNCC in October of 1970.

CUMBERLAND COLLEGE OF TENNESSEE
LEBANON, TENNESSEE

May 13, 1971

Mr. Jim Morris
Bowling Green High School
Bowling Green, Kentucky 42101

Dear Jim:

    As of right now, I do not know where I am going to be coaching next year. I will be glad to have you wherever I go.

    Please don't pass up any good scholarship offers that you might have. The main thing for you to do right now is to graduate.

    I will keep in touch, and I will let you know something as soon as I find out.

          Sincerely,

          Coach Day
          Russ Day
          Director of Athletics

RD:lb

Letter from Cumberland College

L-R: Jim Morris, Steve Carter, Frank Ragland with District and Regional trophies in 1971

Jim with Frank Ragland signing scholarship with Cameron College (Oklahoma). Front, l-r: Opal Morris, Jim Morris, Frank Ragland, Dwight Ragland. Back, l-r: Don Webb, Stan Markham.

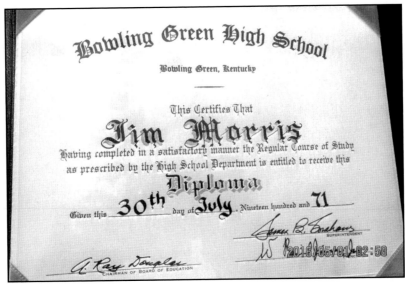

High School diploma... notice the date: July 30th.

Heavy hobby
Former BGH cager into weightlifting

By JIM GROVE
Daily News Sports Writer

Jim Morris can chuckle when someone complains of a weight problem. Although he weighs 270 pounds, his only weight problem comes in the form of a barbell.

So far, that hasn't been a problem to Morris, an ex-Bowling Green High basketball star. Although he has been competing for less than two years, he has won four of five meets in the super heavyweight class, for those in excess of 242 pounds.

Actually, Morris is probably remembered most for his antics on the basketball court. He averaged almost 17 points a game on BGH's 1972 team which finished second in the region to Franklin-Simpson.

He also played basketball (and lifted weights) at various junior colleges and universities before deciding to concentrage only on weight-lifting. But he says weight-lifting didn't influence his decision to quit basketball competitively.

"It's kind of a mystique that lifting weights hurts you in basketball," Morris said. "It's just according to the exercises you do. There's no way weight-lifting will do anything but help you."

"I go out right now and play basketball on Sunday," he said. "I shoot just as well as I did in high school. You've just got to have a touch—I play it all the time."

The truth is Morris spends most of his time working on his weights. His best lift in competition came at the Kentucky Weightlifting Championships last year when he had a 600 total (260 snatch, 340 clean and jerk) to win. At the Mid-South Weightlifting Championships last month in Chattanooga, Morris set a meet record with a two-day total of 580 (255 snatch, 325 clean and jerk).

"The only thing I care about is that I want to improve," he said. "The first meet I didn't go to win, I just planned on being in the top three. It just so happened that I won it."

Morris started lifting when a friend told him about it as a junior in high school, and he's been doing it ever since. He has grown only one inch since then, but has gained 65 pounds.

"It's very individual. I enjoy the individual thing," Morris said. "In team sports, if you have a good game it doesn't necesarily mean you'll win. If I succeed I do, if I don't, I don't."

"It comes to a point...one reason it's so great is because when you step up on a platform, you know there's no-one else to depend on," he said. "You can't say that someone didn't block or someone didn't set a pick. It's you."

Morris has had a best in training of 635 (280 snatch, 355 clean and jerk) and has set a 710 total as his goal. He believes it can be reached.

"A lot is learning how to do it," Morris said. "I try to work to a certain percentage each day, like 80 percent is my maximum in training. I have light days, medium days and heavy days, a cycle like that."

Many of the meets he has won have Olympic hopefuls competing, and Morris is one of them.

"I believe I can, but I'm not going to be disappointed if I don't get there by 80," he said. "There will still be two more I'll have a chance at."

"I'm not going to say that's what I want do. My deal is that I want to enjoy it for a whole bunch of years. I'm not saying it's impossible to go, I'm just going to keep on trying."

After all, actions speak louder than words.

Bowling Green Daily News article

The Cameron College team. Frank Ragland is #4 on the front row and Jim is #23 on the second row.

Jim with several teammates after transferring to Vol State in Gallatin, Tennessee, 1972.

Volunteer State Pioneers

Basketball 1973-74

President - Dr. Hal Ramer
Chairman of Athletics - Jess Mallory

Coach - Richard Moore
Assistant - Bill Higdon
Manager - Corky Carter

Men

NO. W – R	NAME	POS.	CLASS	HT.	WT.	HOME	1ST HALF	2ND HALF	TOTAL
14 - 15	Ron Carter	G	F	6-2	160	Clarksville			
44 - 45	Steve Davidson	F	S	6-6	185	Goodlettsville			
34 - 35	James Ellis	G-F	S	6-2	170	Glasgow, Ky.			
24 - 25	James Haddox	G-F	S	6-1	167	Franklin			
52 - 53	Jerry Hall	F	F	6-3	205	Goodlettsville			
40 - 41	Stan Johnson	G-F	F	6-3	172	Nashville			
31 - 31	Larry Knight	F	S	6-2½	189	Nashville			
20 - 21	Tyree Ligon	G	F	6-0	163	Gallatin			
22 - 23	Ray Merrell	G	F	6-0	163	Nashville			
54 - 55	Jim Morris	C-F	S	6-6	225	Bowling Gr., Ky.			
42 - 43	Doug Shearon	G	S	5-11	161	Ashland City			
32 - 33	Bill Sinks	F	S	6-1	171	Hendersonville			
50 - 51	John Sublett	C	S	6-6	205	Nashville			
10 - 11	Freddie Taylor	G	F	6-0	147	Bowling Gr., Ky.			

Vol State roster, note Jim's size.

In the beginning, Jim didn't always wrestle in front of sold out arenas.

In 1981, Jim returned for his 10-year class reunion at Bowling Green High School. Seated front and center, he was voted by his classmates "Most Changed for the Better!"

Jim wrestling as "Big Jim" Morris in 1982.

Jim in early day match at the Jaycee Pavilion in Bowling Green.

OFFICIAL PROGRAM

SPARWOOD

Thursday, November 3, 1983

BAD NEWS ALLEN
vs
MR. HITO

KERRY 'BUSTER' BROWN
vs
SHUNJI TAKANO

TAG TEAM MATCH
Butch Moffat & Cal Manson
vs
Jim Morris & Randy Webber

STEVE LOGAN
vs
K. Y. WAKAMATSU

Official program

Jim in a match in Bowling Green.

It was Jerry "The King" Lawler who came up with the Harley Davidson persona in 1983.

Jim enters the ring with partner Dirty Rhodes in a match in Memphis, April of 1984.

November 26, 1984

Mr. James Morris
729A Gordon Avenue
Bowling Green, Kentucky 42101

Dear Jim:

Enclosed find the following items:

1) Agreement. Would you please read the enclosed agreement, sign it, and return it to our office at your earliest convenience. Thereafter, you will be made available a copy for your records.

2) Plane ticket. Your plane ticket indicates that you will arrive in New York at 11:01 A.M. at Laguardia Airport. We will see to it that somnone picks you up and brings you to the office here in Greenwich, where George Scott will meet you and speak to you.

If you have any problems whatsoever before next Tuesday, do not hesitate to call. Thank you very much.

Very truly yours,

Howard Finkel
Titan Sports, Inc.

COPY: Mr. George Scott

Jim's letter from Titan Sports (WWF) in November of 1984.

14. Life Insurance. Promoter shall have the right, at its election, to obtain life or other insurance upon Wrestler in such amounts as it may determine and at Promoter's cost and expense, including but not limited to insurance against the failure of Wrestler to appear and to participate in any Event; Wrestler shall have no right, title or interest in any such insurance. Wrestler agrees to cooperate and assist in Promoter's obtaining such insurance, including submitting to such physical or other examinations of Wrestler as may be required to obtain such insurance and by preparing, signing, and delivering such applications and other documents as may reasonably be required.

15. Indemnification. Wrestler shall indemnify Promoter and Promoter's licensees, assignees and affiliates and their respective officers, directors, employees and representatives and hold each of them harmless from any claims, demands, liabilities, actions, costs, suits, proceedings or expenses (including without limitation reasonable attorneys fees and expenses) incurred by any of them by reason of the breach or alleged breach of any warranty, undertaking representation, agreement or certification made or entered into herein or hereunder by Wrestler and/or Wrestler's conduct within or around the ring, hallways, dressing rooms, parking lots or other areas within or in the immediate vicinity of the facilities where Promoter has scheduled Events for Wrestler.

16. Independent Contractor. Nothing contained in the Agreement shall be construed to constitute Wrestler as a partner or joint venturer of Promoter, nor shall Wrestler have any authority to bind Promoter in any respect. Wrestler shall render his services hereunder as an independent contractor. Wrestler will execute, and hereby irrevocably appoints Promoter his attorney-in-fact to execute if Wrestler refuses to do so, any instruments requested by Promoter to accomplish or confirm the foregoing.

17. Entire Contract. This Agreement contains the entire understanding of the parties, with respect to the subject matter hereof, and supersedes all previous verbal and written agreements; there are no other agreements, representations, or warranties not set forth herein, with respect to the subject matter hereof. This Agreement may not be changed or altered except by an agreement in writing signed by Promoter and Wrestler.

18. Assignment. Promoter shall have the right to assign, license or transfer any or all of the rights granted to it hereunder to any person, firm or corporation and if any assignee shall assume in writing Promoter's obligations hereunder, Promoter shall have no further obligations to Wrestler hereunder. Wrestler may not assign, transfer or delegate his rights or obligations hereunder and any attempt to do so shall be void.

19. Notices. Any notices required or desired hereunder shall be in writing and sent postage prepaid by certified mail, return receipt requested, or by prepaid telegram addressed as follows (or addressed as the parties may hereafter in writing otherwise designate):

TO PROMOTER:
Titan Sports, Inc.
81 Holly Hill Lane, P.O. Box 4520
Greenwich, Connecticut 06830
Attention: President

TO WRESTLER:

The date of mailing or delivery to the telegraph office shall be deemed to constitute the date of service of any such notice.

20. Choice of Law. This Agreement shall be governed by the laws of the State of Connecticut applicable to contracts entirely made and performed therein.

IN WITNESS WHEREOF, the parties have executed this Agreement on the day and year first above written.

TITAN SPORTS, INC.

By: _~L. McMahon~_
Authorized Officer

_____
(Wrestler) Ring Name

James N. Morris
(Legal Name)

-4-

Agrement signed by Jim Morris and Linda McMahon.

Dale Mann locks up his boots before a match. It was Mann who helped Jim get his start in wrestling.

Jim with Dr. Tom Harris and his wife Linda in San Diego, 1985.

Jim and his grandmother, Trudy Houchens in Lamb, Kentucky in 1986.

While Jim was sidelined with his injury, he "managed" Uncle Elmer. Here they are with Vince McMahon.

Jim and Uncle Elmer

Hulk Hogan and Jim

Jim at ringside taunting the competition

Hulk Hogan presents Jim with a real pair of wrestling boots after Jim saved him from a bad haircut at the hands of Bobby "The Weasel" Heenan and company.

Jim with Haiti Kid and Little Beaver, his WrestleMania III tag team partners.

Jim plays his guitar as Gorilla Monsoon and Bobby "The Brain" Heenan watch.

Jim and the Godwins.

Andre the Giant applies a choke hold to Jim.

Hulk Hogan makes sure Jim is okay as he goes through some weight training.

Jim, with hat in hand, is congratulated by a fan after a win.

Jim puts his big boot into the ribs of Boris Zhukof.

Jim clamps a vicious headlock on King Kong Bundy.

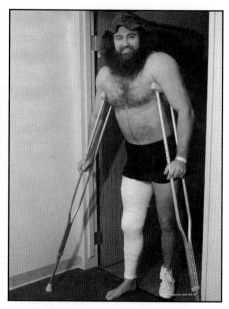

Jim on crutches after surgery.

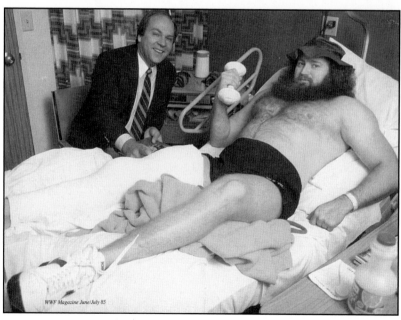

Jim with Dr. Harris after recovering from surgery.

In the meantime, teammate Steve Carter had signed to play for Coach Guy Lewis at the University of Houston, who was building a national powerhouse.

"I played with Dwight Jones there, and against Tom Henderson and Otis Birdsong," Carter said. "It was a big deal back then, but later I transferred to Western where I pitched on the baseball team."

Not long after Carter had committed to Houston, Jim and one of his best friends, teammate Frank Ragland, signed basketball scholarships to play at Cameron College in Lawton, Oklahoma. They had enjoyed their recruitment trip and their first airplane ride to the school, and were happy they would play some more basketball together.

At Bowling Green High the two were almost inseparable. With Jim being white and Frank black, they were like brothers from the time they first met.

"We went out for the freshman team together," recalls Ragland. "I was cut and although 'County' made the team, he quit because he never got to play.

"We played basketball all the time together, hustling other guys out of a little money so we could walk over to the old Hill-Motley Lumber Company and buy us a drink and snacks they had just inside the front door. We always had a little change in our pockets. 'County' and I were project boys, walked all over Bowling Green together. That's the way we got around. We didn't have a car."

Both Jim's and Frank's high school basketball careers had been put back on track when Don Webb joined Larry Doughty as his assistant coach the next year after their freshman year.

"The best thing to ever happen in our life was when Coach Webb came along," Frank says. "We didn't care about school, but Coach Webb gave us a chance, and because he did we stayed in school."

And now here they were: two friends, high school teammates sitting at a table at Bowling Green High School, each with pen in hand, Jim flanked by his smiling mother, Opal, and Frank by his brother Dwight, signing scholarship papers for Cameron College. Standing behind them were Don Webb and Stan Markham.

At Cameron, Jim and Frank played for Coach Red Miller, and what a rousing start they had. In a much anticipated intrasquad game, Jim and Frank's White team stunned the highly favored veteran Gold squad 94-85, as each of the Bowling Green freshmen scored 26 points.

"I just stayed one year," Jim said. "Didn't go to class much either. It was a football school, and they wanted the coach to switch my scholarship to football. They fed me like you wouldn't believe. It was all right. There were lots of boots and Skoal."

"Jim was as good as there was for his size," Ragland said. "His jump shot was beautiful, and when we threw it to him he was going to the goal. He was automatic."

Frank, on the other hand, stayed all four years at the NAIA school, becoming a starting point guard.

While many of Jim's early day friends were surprised at what the future held for his friend, Frank was not.

"I really wasn't," Frank laughed. "At Cameron the guys across the hall in the dorm would have fake wrestling matches, blood and all. Jim would join in on the fun. His personality and all was right for it.

"Looking back on it, we wouldn't trade where we lived in Bowling Green or what we did for anything. If Jim hadn't lived where he did he wouldn't appreciate what he has now."

Jim Morris had left Cameron and was now back in Bowling Green, not really sure what he wanted to do with his life, or even if he would play basketball again.

He had continued the weight lifting regimen that he and friend Tommy Hagan had begun a couple of years before, and not only was he now standing six-foot-six, but weighed 225 lbs.

After deciding to give basketball another shot while sitting out before playing at Vol State in Tennessee, Jim had become acquainted with a fellow in Gallatin named Bill Buntin. Buntin was the general manager of radio station WHIN and also involved in an Industrial Basketball League in nearby Portland.

With Jim Morris just wanting to play some while waiting for his eligibility to kick in, Buntin recruited him to play for a team sponsored by a business called Shoe World.

"It worked good for me," says Jim. "They gave us all kinds of shoes and clothes, and heck I'd score 50-60 points against guys that really weren't very good. But I was having fun. Looking back on it, I had a philosophy that if I was any good at all, regardless of the competition I should be able to score 20 points and get 10 rebounds in every game. I could get 10 points a game just on hustle alone."

"I laid out that year and then played with Volunteer State," Jim said. "That was in the 1973-74 basketball season. I just had the one year there."

But what a year it was, averaging 24 points and 14 rebounds.

At Vol State Jim met another student, and soon after fell in love with and married. Though it was an out of race marriage for both, Jim never missed a beat, nor felt it was all that unusual for him even though it was in the '70s. After all, he had grown up with his best friends and neighbors being black, and Gayle Hill and her family were okay with it, too.

"She was from Gallatin, Tennessee, and her daddy was a preacher," says Jim. "She was the oldest of nine children, pretty, really smart and a good student."

Next came a brief stint at Lee College in Cleveland, Tennessee, and then one semester at Georgetown College in Georgetown, Kentucky.

"I really liked Coach (Jim) Reid at Georgetown. He really knew the game and they had some tough rugged guys I enjoyed banging with," Jim laughed. "But someone at the school said I was there illegally. It turned out not to be a good situation for me or Coach Reid, so I left."

Once again Jim had returned home, where he still planned to play some more college basketball. No, not at Western, but this time at a start-up program at Bowling Green Business College.

The school's director brought in Dave Denton to build and coach the team. Well-known in the area, Denton had been an All-State player at old College High in Bowling Green before becoming a star player at Georgia Tech. The thinking was, a basketball team would draw publicity for the school that would lead to increased enrollment.

Denton signed a few of the locals that included Jim Morris, and put together a schedule that featured games against several Ohio Valley Conference jayvee squads, Athletes In Action, Trevecca College and the University of Louisville jayvees.

"We played Trevecca on our home court at St. Joe Gym," Jim said. "I had 43 against them and their fans were calling me a criminal because I'd been at so many different schools."

Jim continued: "I scored 36 here against Louisville's jayvees, but when we went back there to play them in Freedom Hall I was just getting over some torn ligaments from a game against the Job Corp. Denny Crum (U of L coach) was there to watch us. I didn't have a good game because of my injury."

Unfortunately, the team folded after one year, and now it did indeed look like Jim's basketball days were over.

As far back as he could remember he had played basketball, bordering on being a "gym rat." The itch was still there to play even it if was knocking around in the pickup games at Diddle Arena. Over the years he had played against the likes of Hilltopper stars Granville Bunton, Mike Odemns, and even Clem Haskins, while holding his own.

But now the time had come in his life at the age of 22 to make some decisions. Deep down Jim knew his competitive basketball days were coming to a close. He had played the game at a fairly high level, leaving a footprint at least in Bowling Green, Kentucky and northern Tennessee, and in the process he had managed to mix basketball, and his new found love of weight lifting.

"When I saw something I wanted I locked in on it. It's all about focus and intensity," he said. "I always knew I didn't want to get up and go to a factory or even an office every day."

Jim had at one time taken a job in a tobacco warehouse. "Didn't last a day," he recalled. "Breathing that air couldn't be good. I wouldn't even sweep the floors."

He was not opposed to working hard, but Jim, still searching for what he might want to do the rest of his life was not something he spent a great deal of time worrying about.

"I had little jobs here and there most of my life," he said. "I worked at the Squirt Bottling Company on Church Street when I was in high school. And I'll tell you the worst job I ever had, and I mean ever, was at a meat packing place out on Richardsvile Road. I was in college and needed the job. It wasn't that the job was too tough, but it was what you had to see and smell. I've never seen anything like it. Couldn't stand the thought of eating bacon for a while…those poor hogs. I lasted four hours."

Jim began to concentrate more and more on his weight lifting, even to the point that it had almost become an obsession. His neighborhood friend, Tommy Hagan, had lit a fire in Jim several years before that instead of burning out, just kept getting brighter.

"I loved working out and exercising," he said. "I figured why not do something that involved exercise and get paid for it?"

By now Jim Morris had become almost a daily fixture in the Western Kentucky University weight room in Smith Stadium. Even though he had never gone to a class at the University, he seemed to be accepted by everyone associated with the school.

Bill "Yogi" Meadors was one of the teachers in the Physical Education Department at the college, and became acquainted with Jim.

"Dr. Burch Oglesby was responsible for the weight room," Meadors offered. "It was the only one we had. Everybody used it…football team, track, students, you name it. It was a busy place. Burch would let some of the non-students come in and big Jim was one of them."

"I became good friends with Jesse Stuart. He was a world-class shot-putter," says Jim. "We lifted and challenged each other every day."

It was this relationship Jim forged with Stuart and his brothers, John, Howard and Brill that would last a lifetime. Jesse had hopes of being an Olympian, and the Glasgow, Kentucky native took to big Jim quickly.

"The Stuart's showed me about the technique of lifting," Jim said. "They were my idols, strong, fast, and great weightlifters."

All of the Stuart brothers were characters, each in their own way.

"They were special people," Jim laughs. "Brill was the oldest and he could punt a football so far it was said the Colts wanted him to kick for them. He had a beard down to his knees and they called him Big T for big trip, which stood for LSD.

"Brill came by to see my mother and me one time. He had a hat like Clint Eastwood would wear in a movie. It was leather and he traded it to me for a beret I had. The Stuart's dad, Dr. John Stuart, was a chiropractor and had bought it in Mexico."

That hat would later become a part of the Hillbilly Jim persona when he entered the ring with it on.

"He was a tall, skinny kid, maybe nine or ten years old," Jesse Stuart laughed when recalling the first time he saw Jim. "The next time I saw him was when he came up to the weight room at Western, maybe 1972. He wanted to learn Olympic style lifting. He wasn't into all the Pop-Eye stuff, curls and all. We were power lifting and we taught him the right way."

Jesse did indeed do things the right way. The Glasgow native still holds the Kentucky High School shot-put record, and for 40 years he held the national prep mark. His 68-3 toss is still the Western Kentucky University record he set in 1975. Stuart actually made the 1980 Olympic team, but that was the year President Jimmy Carter called for a boycott.

85

"Later I had a few throws of 69-feet, that's my best," he said.

The next time the Stuart family saw their friend Jim Morris he was climbing into the wrestling ring out of the crowd to help Hulk Hogan.

"We couldn't believe it," Stuart recalled. "My brother John and I saw this big guy dressed in overalls climbing in the ring. It was big Jim."

Jim Morris was no longer the tall skinny kid they called "Allen County," and no longer did he wear the dark horn-rimmed glasses. Those were replaced with contact lens when he played at Vol State a few years earlier.

Jim now stood 6-foot-7 and weighed 260 lbs..

"Burch Oglesby was good to me," Jim continued. "And I tried to do my part also. Gene Keady (Western basketball coach) liked me and ask me if I'd work with some of his players. I remember Craig McCormick (future 6-10 basketball star). He was like a young giraffe."

As students came and went in the Smith Stadium weight room, big Jim always seemed to be there. If he wasn't lifting he was "spotting" for friends who did. With his size and strength many would often spend time watching him lift. With his grunts, groans and screams, Jim Morris' accomplishments were shared with everyone in the room.

There were times during the year when Western was shut down, so Jim turned to the House of Fitness where his weight lifting numbers became legendary. It was here that he realized the importance of proper technique. It was here that he began to prepare for weight lifting competition, even toying with the idea of participating in the Olympic Trials.

Jim had competed against several lifters who were considered Olympic hopefuls. And he won. Back in the mid-'70s he told a newspaper, "I believe I can, but I'm not going to be disappointed if I don't get there by '80 (Olympics). I'm just going to keep on trying."

He had every reason to be confident. Now weighing 270, he won the Kentucky Weightlifting Championship when he totaled 600 pounds, with 260 in the snatch and 340 in the clean and jerk. A few months later in Chattanooga he set a meet record at the Mid-South Championship with a 580 total (255 snatch, 325 clean and jerk). Both of those numbers were below his personal training best of 635 (280 and 355).

In spite of Jim's success, some considered his height to be a detriment in weightlifting. "My height didn't help me," he says. "Most successful lifters were shorter."

Although Jim was devoting almost an obsessive amount of time in the weight room, he still had not lost his love of two important things in his life: basketball and music.

"I had been playing both since I can remember," he says. "So they weren't going anywhere." But remember, he had been only lifting the iron since his junior year of high school, just not at the level he now was.

"I heard some people say you couldn't lift and play ball, too," he said. "I don't believe that. It's just according to the exercises you do."

Weightlifting by day with an occasional pick-up basketball game, Jim needed to have a source of income. It didn't take much for him to meet his personal needs by working here and there as a bouncer in several local night spots, as well as for a liquor store, and with a mobile home sales company.

"It was not always pretty," he says. "But by this time I was 22 and had a daughter. I had to make some money. The liquor store where I worked was the only one in Bowling Green where you could come in and drink. Not sure it was legal, but we did it. Every now and then I'd have to lift a customer up like a mama cat and set him outside. We also ran credit there, too. I know we weren't supposed to, but we did it. Some would run up big bills and then die."

While there were several Bowling Green businesses that required bouncers to keep order, Jim Morris was the most visible. Anyone would have been insane, drunk or sober, to challenge his authority. But sometimes they did.

There were stories about Jim. One quickly spread that while he was working at one establishment he had an altercation with one of the over-served customers, and un-ceremonially escorted him out. The next day the brother of the man came by and confronted Jim, saying he didn't like the way his brother was treated, and was there to even the score. Without getting up from the bar stool he was sitting on, Jim one-punched the guy, knocking him to the floor.

Whether or not it actually happened that way is not important. What was important is that stories like this added to his reputation. No, Big Jim was no one to mess with.

"Ever now and then," he recalled, "Alcohol can make you bullet-proof, and once in a while I'd have to stamp somebody out. I never lost a challenge. If you lost as a bouncer, you'd be done in the business. I had very few fights because I was pretty good at talking and could usually calm the situation. But when I couldn't, I was ready, and could take care of things. I was the highest paid bouncer in town, making $100 a night. That was good money back then for three or four hours of work."

Jim still played pick-up games on Sundays, and says though he was still lifting competitively, he could shoot a basketball as well as he did at the top of his game.

With basketball no longer an everyday focus for him, and weight-lifting occupying more and more of his time, he couldn't dream big enough to know how big of a turn his life was about to take.

Chapter Seven

Now standing 6-foot, 7-inches and weighing 280 lbs., Jim Morris had taken on a whole new persona. He had always had a big, outgoing personality, but now he had the physical presence to match. And it was both of these that opened the door and allowed Jim to walk through it.

While working out at a Bowling Green fitness center in 1978, he met Bruce Swayze. Swayze lived in nearby Franklin, Kentucky, but drove to Bowling Green on a regular basis to workout. It was in an effort to maintain a physical conditioning he had attained as a professional wrestler a few years earlier.

It didn't take long for Swayze to befriend big Jim, asking if he had ever thought about getting into the wrestling business.

"Of course I had seen wrestling on TV" says Jim. "When I was young I'd stay with my grandparents, Henry and Trudy Houchens in Lamb, Kentucky, and we'd watch it on Saturday night. It was a Nick Gulas promotion…lasted a half hour. My granddad Henry would get so worked up watching it that he'd get his knife out. My grandmother told him to settle down or she'd turn the TV off. It was then that I learned the power of a woman."

Bill Buntin, Jim's basketball friend in Gallatin, Tennessee, also had a contact involved in the wrestling game. Tojo Yamamoto at one time had been a relatively big name in the sport, and Buntin had met him through his connection as general manager of WHIN Radio. He arranged for Jim to meet Tojo at the Nashville Fairgrounds for a brief introduction to wrestling, and to see if it was anything Jim would like to pursue.

"He actually tried to stretch me (term for hurt) when we got in the ring," Jim says. "I met with him a couple of times and then I realized he was bullshitting me. He passed himself off as being from Japan, which was all part of his character. He was actually from Hawaii, but playing on the World War II Tojo's name made him a villain in the ring. He was a popular wrestler."

And speaking of Japan, in a bit of a sidebar, Vince McMahon, Sr., was somewhat involved in the infamous side show that took place in 1976 between boxing champion Muhammad Ali and Japanese pro-wrestler, Antonio Inoki.

Decades later it is still difficult to see how Ali could have been talked into such a match, much less a scheduled 15-rounder…and in Japan.

Boxing promoter, Bob Arum, who put it together, wanted to make sure the "show" was just that…a show, and that Ali would be in no danger of jeopardizing his career.

Supposedly, Arum went to McMahon, Sr., (before Jr. was in charge) who was considered a top shelf wrestling promoter. The story goes that McMahon scripted a plan that called for Ali to pin Anoki against the ropes and continuously pummel him with body blows that weren't as hard as they looked.

The story continues:

Anoki was to have a razor hidden on him so he could cut himself and real blood would begin to flow. McMahon's script called for Ali to plead with the referee to stop the fight. At this point Ali would turn his back on Anoki at which time the wrestler would jump on Ali's back, throw him to the mat and pin him.

To really set the crowd off and the thousands watching on closed-circuit throughout the United States, Ali was to scream "It's Pearl Harbor all over again!"

The hitch to it all, however, was that Anoki and his people thought the match was going to be for real, and he had a strategy of almost immediately falling on his back in the middle of the ring. For fifteen rounds he kicked at Ali, often landing vicious blows to the champ's legs, while Ali landed very few punches.

When it was all over the referee, who had been in on McMahon's original plan, declared the match a draw as a boisterous Tokyo crowd showed their displeasure.

It was said at the time Ali suffered enough damage from those hundreds of Anoki's kicks to his thighs, that his future might be in jeopardy.

Michael St. John was another radio guy and a friend of Buntin's. He not only was a broadcaster, but was also connected to the local and regional wrestling scene in the South.

"When I first met Jim he was a bouncer at the Brass A in Bowling Green," says St. John. "I was working for (wrestling) promoter Nick Gulas. He was big in Memphis, Nashville, and throughout the South, about 14 states."

St. John's even recalled another hillbilly connection to professional wrestling.

"Gulas, and (promoter) Roy Welch, had the Scuffling Hillbillies back in the 1960s," he said. "They went by Rip and Slim and their manager was Cousin Alford. They really drew good crowds, and they're finishing move was the possum stomp."

Jim was thinking about it all. Knowing that other than recreation, his basketball was over. And though he was really into the sport of weightlifting, he was smart enough to know the financial stability of it was limited. This wrestling thing may not be so bad after all. In fact, it would mesh into the weights almost seamlessly.

But it took a happenchance meeting at a Bowling Green movie theater with a man from Jamestown, Kentucky, some 60 miles away, to push Jim over the edge.

"He asked me if I was Jim Morris," Jim recalled. "He said his son had seen me work out at Western, and he ask me if I had thought about professional wrestling?" It was Dale Mann, a seasoned veteran of years and years in the sport, mostly spent in small time promotions throughout the area performing in front of a couple of hundred people at the most.

Earlier, Bruce Swayze had told Jim that if he wanted to go forward with it, he needed to get trained. And then, as if a movie script was being written, Dale Mann showed up. The perfect storm in the life of Jim Morris seemed to be developing.

"Dale Mann was a tough, tough guy," says Jim. "I met him out at Lampkin Park in the Jaycee Pavilion in Bowling Green and worked out a little. He was in his late 40s, 6-foot-3, about 255 lbs., and he really knew the game. Right off he taught me about breathing in the ring. If you stay tense and tight and not relaxed you'll blow-up (term for not being able to last).

Mann then introduced Jim to Lanny Kean, (who would later become Cousin Junior) and went by the name of Luscious Lanny. He had been a staple to the area wrestling scene for a while, and Mann thought it would be a good test for Jim to get out of Bowling Green and do it for "real."

"I had only three or four training sessions," Jim said. "Tojo (Yamamoto) wanted me to think it would take a long time before I'd ever be ready for a match. Some guys, he said, take six months or more."

But now, in the spring of 1980, here was Big Jim Morris from Bowling Green facing off against Luscious Lanny Kean from Las Vegas, Nevada, in the National Guard Armory in Glasgow, Kentucky, in front of 150 fans.

"He was about 240 lbs. and let me throw him around like a rag doll," Jim recalls. "We did it all, flying mares, you name it. And guess what? He wasn't from Vegas at all. That's what they did back then to create more interest. Who would be excited about me wrestling some guy from Jamestown? I got paid $50."

Jim was ready, but Mann wanted to put his protégé through another test.

"It was at the Jaycee Pavilion in Bowling Green, and I was introduced as Big Jim Morris. We were scheduled for two out of three falls with a one hour time limit, and one hour is a lot of time to be wrestling. I won the first fall, Dale the second, and then time ran out, so it was a draw. We did a Broadway (term for doing the entire show)."

As Jim's relationship with Mann continued to evolve, it was Swayze, wrestling under the name of "Beautiful Bruce," who realized that Jim was a natural. His size alone was impressive, but when combined with athletic ability and flexibility, his new friend thought there might be a star in the making.

Bruce Swayze knew the ropes and the rings. He had been at it since giving up an ambition of playing hockey in his native Ontario, Canada when he was much younger. It was wrestling, he decided, that would be his meal ticket. From New York to Florida to Nashville and throughout the country, he wrestled.

"It can be a lucrative business and open doors outside the ring," he said. "But it's a tough, tough way to make a living."

Early on, there weren't many lucrative nights for Jim. There were several matches he wasn't paid at all. "Because the crowd was so small, there wasn't enough gate for a payout," Jim said.

"We'd wrestle some nights in front of 15 people. With small crowds it was difficult to call our "spots" to each other," Jim said. "I figured if I could entertain 15, Madison Square Garden would be a snap. The most I ever made with Dale was $100 for a match."

In the smaller wrestling venues such as high school gyms, V.F.W. halls or local recreation centers, it was a big deal when wrestlers came to town. Unfortunately, these smaller wrestling promotions were unable to keep the fans far enough away from the ring in order to provide adequate protection for both the fans and the combatants. Here's an example of a warning in one of those smaller promotions:

FANS WARNED AGAINST INVOLVEMENT

Because of a recent incident in which a spectator at a wrestling match interfered with a wrestler as the latter left the ring, resulting in police having to act to protect the fan from injury, spectators are warned to "please don't become involved with the wrestlers." It's too dangerous.

Professional wrestlers have to be tough to take the hard knocks that are regular fare in their sport, and keep in top shape. Their ability to absorb hard, physical punishment is well known, and is matched by very few average citizens or even athletes from other sports.

Also, because he is probably already "heated up" as a result of the hard-hitting action in which he has been engaged in his legitimate bout, a wrestler can hardly be blamed if his temper is at the hair-trigger point. For an outsider to try to be a hero by interfering in such a situation is asking for trouble and injury. "It just isn't worth it."

Not long after, Jim made his way to Calgary, Canada, where he hooked up with Stu Hart who headed the Stampede Wrestling organization. Hart was the patriarch of the famous wrestling Hart family, with Bret and Owen being the most well known. Stu Hart had participated in more than 5,000 matches in his career, and he, too, was impressed by the big Kentuckian's size.

In one of Jim's few matches he had in Canada, he was featured in a tag team match with Randy Webber against Butch Moffat and Cal Manson. He wrestled under the Jim Morris name, and in the printed program that night Stu Hart wrote that Jim was new to Canada, and "I still have to see if he has the stamina to be a wrestler."

(Owen Hart died in 1999, in a freak zip line type accident while entering the ring in Kansas City's Kemper Arena.)

"They were going to make my Big Jim character a tough oil field worker, but it never really got off the ground, because my mother got sick and I went back to Bowling Green," he says.

At the time Jim didn't know it, but he was about to catch a break that would vault him to another tier. At this point of his relatively new profession nothing had been discussed about any kind of insurance in case of an injury. Nor was there a mention on how his body would feel in 25 years. He didn't mind. Big Jim was on his way. He was well aware of the American Wrestling Association in Memphis headed up by wrestling kingpin Jerry "The King" Lawler. Soon the two had connected.

Jim now had a bushy head of hair and a full beard to match, and Lawler saw him as a motorcycle guy. The two went to a Harley Davidson dealership in Memphis and Lawler dressed him out in motorcycle ware from head to toe. It mattered little to Jim that he had never even ridden on a Harley, much less driven one. What mattered was that Harley Davidson, the wrestler, was born.

"Jerry bought it all that day—hat, goggles, vest, shirts, gloves, chaps, you name it, he bought it," he said. "It was so nice of him to buy it, but later I was informed I had to pay him back."

It was with the American Wrestling Association that Jim saw a real opportunity to make a name for himself. It was here he felt he could learn what big time professional wrestling was all about.

Lawler had brought a lot of publicity to, not only himself, but to the business when his "made for television" encounter with comedian Andy Kaufman was so realistic, even host Dave Letterman on NBC wasn't so sure.

One of the major stars of the TV series "Taxi," Kaufman was well known for his off-the-wall humor that could rival that of Robin Williams. To further show his unpredictability in the early '80s, he went on Saturday Night Live accompanied by wrestling legend Nature Boy Buddy Rogers and issued a challenge to any woman in the audience to a wrestling match. In a barrage of silly talk, he declared himself as the inter-gender wrestling champion, while using the forum to challenge one of wrestling's biggest stars at the time, King Jerry Lawler, to a match.

Kaufman had made a name for himself on the television series Taxi, and carried over his schtick into other entertainment venues. In poking fun at wrestling he began wrestling women, proclaiming himself as a champion of women's wrestling. Lawler didn't take kindly of Kaufman's taunts and invited him to Memphis to one of his matches.

The two agreed to appear together at the Memphis Coliseum on April 5, 1982. It didn't take long before Lawler lifted the comedian into the air and drove him head first into the ring in a wrestling move referred to as a pile driver. With Kaufman's body sprawling motionless, no one was laughing, Lawler then picked him up and repeated the move.

With Kaufman's entertainment notoriety, it wasn't long before Letterman had picked up on it and invited the pair to appear on his show. Lawler's rough and tumble edge meshed perfectly with Kaufman's somewhat mealy-mouthed, quirky personality.

Of course the Memphis melee was shown, and once again right there on the Letterman set Lawler aggressively smacked Kaufman in the face, neck brace and all.

Letterman himself appeared stunned. Lawsuits were threatened by way of profanities from Kaufman. All very believable.

For Kaufman it only added to his ability to grasp the far-reaches of his mind to entertain, while for Lawler it reinforced his wrestling character as a "heel."

By the way, their Letterman's appearance was named "All-Time Top 60 television moments in TV history."

Jim Morris now felt good about his new situation in professional wrestling. He was on the move with Lawler.

"They hooked me up with a tag-team partner, Roger Smith," he said. "He was a real veteran who had, over the years, performed as one of those masked guys. The name he went by was Dirty Rhodes (a play on wrestler Dusty Rhodes' name). We were good guys."

Harley Davidson and Dirty Rhodes were a hit. Though Smith had been pretty much a journeyman most of his career, he had a reputation of being difficult to deal with, according to Jim. "He was a tough guy and a lot of people were scared of him. There were times when a swat team had to go to his house to extract him."

Smith had been mostly an undercard for the majority of his career, and Jim says it was guys like him that were really tough.

"In reality the warm-up guys were the toughest," he added. "The big stars sometimes couldn't whip anyone's ass."

Jim and Roger were driving 2,000 miles a week performing in Evansville, Indiana; Lexington, Kentucky; Nashville and Jackson, Tennessee; and Jonesboro, Arkansas, all the while returning every Monday night to wrestle in the Memphis Coliseum. By now he had made Memphis his home.

For Jim, it was an educational process.

"Roger educated me on the inside stuff, how to keep from getting hurt. It was the little things I learned from him," he said.

But then Smith began to question his pay. Although the tag team received $1,000 for a main event, he wanted more.

"He left," says Jim. "He was my partner, so I left, too."

Jim was on the road constantly, spending little time at home with his young family. He had set his sights now on a professional wrestling career, and he had now gotten a little taste of the money to be made. He was going for it, knowing this was an opportunity for him to at least financially provide for his family, and his mother in Bowling Green.

"I was gone all of the time," he said. "I always made sure Gayle, my kids, and mother were okay." "I had become so used to being out on the road that when I was home I was stressed out. That's what I had become used to."

For Jim and his family, in a dysfunctional sort of way, it seemed to work.

Chapter Eight

*N*o one has ever accused Jim Morris of being dumb. And they weren't about to now, even if he had parted ways with Jerry Lawler's Memphis wrestling organization. He wasn't about to walk away from a paycheck with no place else to go.

He had received an education while working with Lawler and it wasn't in a classroom, and not necessarily the ring either.

"Lawler was one smart son-of-a-bitch," Jim says. "And he was a master in the ring." And then taking a poke at King Lawler's health habits, Jim offered that Lawler drove by lots of health clubs, but didn't pass up a Chick-fil-A.

"Lawler's group didn't like the big tough guys," he added. "They liked the good old boys that they could throw around."

One of those in Lawler's stable was his cousin, Wayne Farris, who wrestled as the Honky Tonk Man. "They didn't get along either," Jim said.

But it was big, tough guys that Lawler tried to entice to come to Memphis to help build his brand. And, according to Jim, some did make the trip south, but didn't exactly receive the southern hospitality they thought they would.

"Several big names went down there and lost. They got fast-counted," Jim said. "Hogan, before he was Hulk when he went by Sterling Golden, and Iron Sheik lost there."

But it was Andre The Giant who was the biggest to fall.

"Vince McMahon, Sr., loaned Andre to Memphis from the WWF," continued Jim. "Lawler was in the ring with him and somehow Andre was down on the mat and six or seven midgets ran in and with Lawler they got a fast count from the referee and Andre lost."

Lawler used the "win" to better his position in the wrestling world, and included video in his promotions material of all of the big names going down in defeat in Memphis. They hated Lawler for what he did, and there were actually reports of a hit being put out on the Memphis wrestler.

"We had our differences, but Jerry and I ended up okay," says Jim. "He stayed upset with me for sometime for leaving the AWA for the WWF. Eventually he became a commentator for the WWF, however, he told me I didn't do him right when I went to WWF, but I told him they paid me more money to sit and watch my mailbox than he paid me in Memphis. I give him credit for the vision of Harley Davidson."

In the meantime Jim had maintained a friendship with Bruce Swayze and his wife, Bonnie. In fact, Bonnie had loaned Jim her car to drive to Memphis to meet with Jerry Lawler the first time.

"Bonnie knew who Jim was before I did," says Swayze. "He was working as a bouncer at one of the places in Bowling Green. And then when I saw him working out at the gym, I didn't know what kind of business he was doing, but I knew it was the wrong one."

Bruce Swayze was there at the right time in Jim Morris' life. If he was going to move beyond the success he had while working with Jerry Lawler, it would have to be hooking up with someone like a former wrestler who literally knew the ropes and was willing to take him under his wing.

Swayze had been at it a long time.

At 5'11", 230 lbs., and could bench press 400 lbs., he wrestled from New York to Florida to Nashville from the 1960s into the 80s. He had seen and done it all, and if it was contacts in wrestling you wanted, he had them, too.

The grind of the daily travel, rugged matches, and occasionally dealing with over-zealous fans can, and did, take a toll on Swayze's body.

"It was in the '70s in Durham, N.C., and one of the fans stabbed me in the arm with a potato peeler," he said.

With this knowledge of who Swayze was, Jim was all in when he was invited to go to Tampa "to see what the business was all about."

"I introduced Jim to Eddie Graham, who promoted with NWA (National Wrestling Alliance)," said Swayze. "He met Black Jack Mulligan, J.J. Dillon and a few others. I wanted him to see this was entertainment, flakey as hell. But if he could find his niche, because of his size, he could make a lot of money."

But Swayze wasn't through.

"We went to a "show" at the Nashville Municipal Auditorium," Jim recalled. "The WWF was putting it on. McMahon was buying up all of the talent and lots of them were there that night…Big John Studd, Junkyard Dog, Valentine, Andre, the Harts. It was a packed house."

Jim knew he was in good hands when Swayze led him to the back door of the Civic Center where you have to know someone to get in. And Jim believed it when he and Swayze were welcomed in.

Pat Patterson was one of McMahon's lieutenants and in charge of most of the match scheduling for the WWF, and Swayze quickly introduced Jim Morris to him. "I told Pat the boy is green, willing to learn, and really smart."

Patterson was impressed with Jim's size, but unfortunately their card that night was full. That was okay with Jim because he had brought nothing in the way of wrestling gear with him. However, 20 minutes later Patterson was back and told Big Jim he had found a preliminary slot for him. So trunks and footwear were rounded up and soon Jim Morris, from Bowling Green, Kentucky, was in a WWF wrestling match.

"I actually got all my gear that night from Jimmy Snuka and I wrestled Tommy Heggie," Jim said. "It was a 30 minute time limit. We did our spots and it worked out okay, with no winner."

Patterson liked what he saw and told Jim to be in Memphis at the Cook County Convention Center the next week. Jim was matched against Salvatore Bellomo.

"He was a good guy…a pear-shaped guy," Jim offered. "He did a cartwheel in the ring and then I did one. The crowd went wild."

Bellomo may not have been a champion wrestler, but he knew his way around some of the finest restaurants. The *WF Magazine* featured him in a four page pictorial wearing a chef's hat and apron in the kitchen of Mario's Restaurant in the Bronx.

Patterson told Jim he'd go back to Connecticut and tell Vince McMahon his thoughts about what he'd seen out of Big Jim.

"Vince and his wife called me," says Swayze, who had made the introduction of Jim to Patterson. "They asked me my connection, if I was his agent. I said no. Vince then told me they wanted to sign him."

Swayze had opened the door once again, and this time it wasn't the back door.

Shortly after, Jim was on a plane headed to the New Haven Coliseum to meet Vince McMahon. This time he took along his uniform of the day, the Harley Davidson outfit that Jerry Lawler had branded him with.

"I did a match as Harley Davidson," Jim said. "Vince liked the way I looked."

But for McMahon there was one slight problem with Jim and his ring moniker. And it was a big one.

McMahon was considered a marketing genius. You didn't have to look far to figure that out. Stadiums and arenas were full, television audiences couldn't get enough, and his slick WWF merchandise was flying off the shelves…all because of the product he had developed.

"He told me we'd have to change my name," Jim said. "We can't market the name Harley Davidson. It's already trademarked."

McMahon and a few of his associates, along with Jim, got together after the match away from the arena floor to discuss a name change for the big Kentuckian.

"There was Chief Jay Strongbow, whose real name was Joe Scarpa from Griffin, Georgia. He was as Italian as John Gatti, but looked the part of an Indian chief," laughed Jim. "And George Scott was there, too. He was one of the operations main guys who could hire and fire. He did a lot of Vince's work for him.

"They threw out several names and then Chief says, 'We haven't had a hillbilly for a while'. They mentioned the Scuffling Hillbillies, a tag team from several years ago. They were Kentucky boys who came into the ring barefoot and carrying cowbells."

The group was onto something…something that was about to change James Henry Morris' life forever.

"One of them said, 'how about Hillbilly Jim?'" he says. "Vince looked up and I could tell he liked it."

"They could have made me a pretty-boy," Jim laughed. "But, I didn't care. I just wanted to get my foot in the door and I didn't care how."

Jim Morris was now Hillbilly Jim, and Chief Strongbow, working full time as an agent for the WWF, then asked Jim what town he would be from. Without hesitating, the answer was Mud Lick, Kentucky in Monroe County.

"After I had been doing the Hillbilly thing for a while Vince asked me how I felt about the name," Jim said. "I told him they could dress me up like a green bean with a big string coming out of my head for what they were going to pay me."

Now officially no longer Harley Davidson in the Memphis wrestling territory, Jim was employed by the World Wrestling Federation out of Greenwich, Connecticut.

"They'd fly me from Nashville to New York and limo me to Connecticut. This was in 1983," Jim said. "Can you believe it…1983, and I'd go to Vince's office. He wanted to get to know me. Would I have a problem being on the road? What would my workout schedule be? Heck, working out had become a way of life for me. How good was Vince to me? He was Oz, PT Barnum, he was excited. He wanted to take the WWF to the moon and then the entire universe."

Jim says Vince McMahon spared nothing in making the WWF successful.

"He cut no corners, and anything I did they paid me, even if I wasn't wrestling," he offered. "If anyone got hurt they paid the medical and their salary. Everything Vince said they'd do, they did."

While McMahon and his organization may have been first class, Jim wasn't quite so sure about some of the characters he'd be dealing with up close and personal.

"When I got there in the beginning and getting to know some of the other guys, I realized I'd probably made a mistake," he says looking back to 1983. "Some of these were the worst asshole guys in the world. But I had a choice. I could pack it in and go back to Bowling Green, or hang in there, make myself some good money, and have a future."

Now performing as Hillbilly Jim from Mudlick, Kentucky, the former basketball star was about to embark in an unknown world that was much like a roulette wheel, round and round it goes, where it stops nobody knows.

Chapter Nine

Vince McMahon had a plan for Jim Morris, and it didn't include putting him in the ring…at least not in the beginning. Jim's directions had been to accelerate his workouts and wait for further instruction.

Daily he'd leave his Gordon Avenue home in Bowling Green, and head to B.G. Weight Lifting & Health Equipment, owned by Don Langley, to spend three hours with the weights. He'd already been a regular there for several years, so saying he was working would be a stretch. He lifted and socialized with friends, who were almost as excited as he was at his new-found opportunity in life. But for sure, neither Jim, his family, nor his friends knew exactly what the WWF had in store for Hillbilly Jim.

"First and foremost they were sending me checks," Jim said. "Heck, I'm making more money sitting at home than I did driving 2,000 miles a week working in Memphis."

But then in December 1983, Vince McMahon's plan for Hillbilly Jim was activated. He would never be the same.

"They wanted to brush me up against Hogan and that would give me instant credibility," said Jim. "So when you had the most popular wrestler in the world singing your praises, I couldn't fail."

Jim says that McMahon was in charge of it all. It wasn't something they had to necessarily get Hogan's approval on. It had been pre-determined in meticulous development of the story line.

"Make no mistake about it, as popular as Hulk Hogan was, he was still an employee of the WWF," added Jim.

"The WWF people realized that if I was accepted like a few of the other top tier guys it would take some of the pressure off of Hogan. He was in constant demand and needed some time away now and then.

There were lots of star 'heels', but with me they had another 'baby face' the fans wanted to see."

"Hogan was so good to me and very helpful and generous. We got along great. The vehicle was the WWF, but Hogan drove it."

"They flew me to New York to go to Madison Square and just sit at ringside. They wanted me to be seen, not just by the fans there, but more so for their television production," he said. "They hid me out after I got to New York, and I actually got in line to buy my ticket like everyone else while wearing my overalls and hat."

That's the way the McMahon organization did it. The big hillbilly with the bib overalls, full beard, and wooly hair, was just another wrestling fan.

"This was all part of the show," says Jim. "They wanted to carry it out to make it as real as possible. Chief Strongbow later on didn't want me to wear jewelry or drive a nice car. He was okay for me driving an old pick-up truck."

For the WWF it was all about staying in character. No matter where Jim Morris went, or what he did, he was now Hillbilly Jim.

The rules for being seen in public talking to a rival competitor often resulted in a fine from the WWF. The good guys were called "baby faces," and the bad guys, "heels." They weren't to be seen together in the same restaurant or even a hotel. It only added to the realness of it all. Over the years the business had developed a language of their own, one only they understood.

Kayfabe is a term with several meanings, depending on who you talk to or what you read. You won't find it in a Webster's dictionary either. The unofficial word had its origin from the old carnival days when made-up happenings were passed off as being real.

The entire professional wrestling world since it's beginning was wrapped up in kayfabe.

"If any of us were talking and a mark walked up we'd start talking in kayfabe, carney talk," Jim explained. "Mark was the word we used to describe someone not in the business."

That's how protective wresting in general was of its sport. It all had to look real, and if it looked real, it was real.

When Hillbilly Jim, all 6'7" 300-plus pounds, took his seat on the front row in the Garden that night, he became as much of a focal point for the crowd as did the behemoth men in the ring.

Portraying the fan that he was, he engaged the fans with his good ole boy, down home smile and facial expressions. He even had a few choice words for the bad guys in the ring, when in the hillbilly's opinion, usually supported by several thousand fans, had turned to unscrupulous measures in order to gain an advantage.

With a TV camera panning in for closeup of the big hillbilly, he would project an assortment of facial expressions that made sure all of the world knew he was not happy with what was going on in the ring.

The announcers, Gorilla Monsoon and Lord Alfred Hayes, would orally acknowledge his presence. "Who's the big hillbilly in bib overalls?" They would ask. "He sure is a big boy."

"I'd show up in Philadelphia, New York, and Canada for all of the big tapings," Jim says. "I was everywhere, and the announcers would say, 'there he is again. Who is the big Hillbilly?'"

That was the plan. They (WWF) cooked it for a couple of months and the longer they stirred it, the hotter it got.

"I never wrestled, I just worked out. As far as the fans were concerned, I was just this big old lovable country boy, who really doesn't know a thing about how to wrestle."

The shows were taped at the Mid-Hudson Convention Center in Poughkeepsie, New York, for the North American Market, and then in Bradford and London, Ontario for the Canadian market.

The pot had been stirred for several months, and now it was time to take the lid off and let Hillbilly Jim out. And the way McMahon and his associates had cooked it was pure genius.

There the hillbilly was sitting at ringside in Poughkeepsie, New York, watching Special Delivery Jones being pummeled into near-unconsciousness by one of the most evil forces in the WWF. Ken Patera, a former Olympic medal winning weight lifter, and his partner 6'10", 365-pound Big John Studd, had set Special Delivery up for they're menacing manager Bobby "The Weasel" Heenan to take the same scissors they had used a couple of weeks earlier to shear the locks of none other than Andre The Giant.

The television camera zoomed in on the hillbilly, visibly upset by now at seeing in the ring before him three on one. On his feet pointing toward the ring, those in the arena were encouraging him to help S D out. But wait a minute, he couldn't jump into the fray. He was just a fan.

Just when the deliriously excited fans were wondering where this was going to go, as only McMahon could plot, you ain't seen nothing yet.

With little hope to save Special Delivery's hair, the crowd went insane with what happened next. Out of the dressing room running at full speed was none other than Hulk Hogan, the biggest star in the profession. Diving headfirst under the bottom rope into the ring, Patera, Studd, and the Weasel suddenly had more to worry about than giving SD a haircut.

With huge bodies flying around the ring at breakneck speed and a large pair of scissors still in hand, the three villains turned their attention to the Hulkster. Attacking him from the front and behind, they soon had rendered Hogan ineffective and unable to defend himself.

With Patera and Studd firmly in control as a result of Patera's iron full nelson clamped on The Hulk, Manager Heenan was preparing to do to wrestling's biggest superstar what they had done to Andre…cut his blond hair.

For the hillbilly from Mudlick, it was more than he could take. Almost entering the ring earlier to help Special Delivery, now he had little choice. He could either stand there and let his hero be subjected to the ultimate humiliation, or do something about it.

The decision was easy. Jumping upon the ring's apron and quickly stepping over the top rope, the 6'7", 300-pound hillbilly grabbed The Weasel, sending the scissors flying across the ring. Patera, totally surprised by it all, didn't know what was happening, and just as suddenly Hogan had broken Patera's hold. As quickly as it began, it had now ended with only The Hulkster, and the equally big hillbilly standing together in the ring.

The 4,000 fans were on their feet, screaming for Hogan and their new hero. Hillbilly Jim had been introduced to the wrestling world.

The slick stirring-the-pot of the McMahon wrestling machine had reached the boiling point and the wrestling world was ready to eat.

WF Magazine, the official mouthpiece of the WWF had his face plastered everywhere, and in their publication's own words "Hillbilly Jim" is a folk hero.

Jim's association with Hogan gave him instant credibility. And in an effort to carry on the kayfabe, he had to maintain his image in and out of the ring.

WF Magazine wrote this about Jim:

"Courtesy is as much a virtue in the mountains as bravery...Jim maintains his dignity and manners, treating his tormentors with a politeness they do not deserve. Although their life (mountain men) can be cruel, they have an innate sense of fair play."

The magazine continued:

"The hillbilly boy from Kentucky is also as gritty and rugged as the country where he was born—a land where men earn a better living down in the mines, sometimes never to return to the surface, where gun fire of family feuds echoes in coves and hollows, and hopped-up cars loaded with bootleg shine, roaring over twisting roads by dark of night. The mountain boy may be a gentleman, but as the song says, You don't mess around with Jim."

Jim Morris had never been in a coal mine, none around Mudlick... really didn't know anyone who had, and for sure his family didn't run moonshine at night. It was all part of the show.

And so, too, was the continuation of a "new" friendship with Hillbilly Jim and Hulk Hogan. After all, it was Jim who had rescued the Hulkster from complete humiliation, and now the biggest name in wrestling felt an obligation to share all of his secrets and training methods with the big hillbilly.

The Hulkster was well aware that Jim (in character) had acquired much of his prodigious strength, developed since boyhood by splitting logs for the fire, plowing stony fields behind stubborn mules, and for a time, working with a jackhammer and shovel in the bowels of a coal mine.

Hogan, according to all of the WWF propaganda, was going to teach Hillbilly Jim about the technique of lifting weights and eating healthy.

With the raw strength of a grizzly wrapping his outstretched arms around a hapless victim in a bear hug, Hogan felt Jim needed to become more sophisticated with his wrestling skills.

"Hogan and I were videoed and photographed in set-up training sessions," Jim laughed. "They had him showing me a proper diet, how to lift weights, and even him showing me where to mark an X on my wrestling contract, since I couldn't write my own name. The truth was I could lift more weight than Hulk Hogan."

Jim Morris was playing the role. He was an "overnight" sensation, imitating his Jethro Bodine Beverly Hillbilly character even better than Max Bear, Jr., did.

"I actually studied his character, and copied a lot of what he said and how he said it," laughed Jim. "Maybe Jethro wasn't the smartest, but he was a genius in a lot of ways. That's what I tried to get across, even to the point of being surprised at my own strength."

Of course Hillbilly Jim was quick to give proper credit for his accomplishments to hard work and eating pickle paw-paws, deviled hawk eggs, bar-b-que raccoon tail, possum fritters, and gopher stew.

Rarely did Hillbilly Jim show his anger, but he would say on occasion, "I was so mad I felt like a weasel running in soft dirt."

Remembering what he had told Chief Strongbow and Vince McMahon months earlier about how they could dress him up like a green bean for what they were paying him, Jim Morris had jumped head first into the top tier of professional wrestling and its biggest stage.

Gone were the small high school gym days when he hoped enough people would show up to pay for gas to get back home. Gone, too, was the Harley Davidson gig, albeit, he was beholding to Jerry Lawler's creativeness for the hook.

But not gone were the memories of his mother's struggle to provide for him and brother, Dwight. And neither were his thoughts about those tent revivals back in Kentucky.

Locked inside of his huge body were voices still shouting at him to never forget how he had gotten to where he was at such a relatively young age in a sport that forced him to grow up fast.

Hillbilly Jim had arrived!

Chapter Ten

There was very little afterthought from Jim at just how long this ride would last. He had, as he would say, brushed against Hulk Hogan, and that meant acceptance.

The scary part of it all is that his career could have ended before it got started, if those large, sharp scissors he knocked from Bobby Heenan's hand while rescuing Hogan, had wound up inadvertently stabbing or cutting him.

"We never discussed the danger of those scissors beforehand," Jim said in looking back on it. "Back then no one gave a crap about stuff like that. It was the show."

Jim was back in Poughkeepsie, a few weeks later for his first official match. After all, he had now been trained sufficiently enough by the Hulkster so that he was ready to go it alone.

"My first match was against Terry Gibbs," Jim recalled. "I bear-hugged him and won the match. Hulk was there and immediately jumped into the ring and presented me with my very own wrestling boots."

The fans couldn't get enough of the boy from Kentucky. His aw-shucks demeanor, and ever-present smile made him the most likable personality in all of wrestling. Some thought his popularity would rival that of Hogan. And that's what Vince McMahon had hoped for.

Not only was McMahon a marketing genius, but he was also a bean counter. And in this case the beans he was counting were green, which is also the color of money.

Before long Hillbilly Jim was booked into Madison Square Garden, the Mecca of anything dealing with sports. He was paired against a Canadian, Sgt. Rene Goulet, who later became an agent to several wrestlers.

By now, Jim had developed a "signature" move that usually resulted in a win. His massive shoulders, developed from a lifetime of weight lifting, and a 64-inch chest, combined with a 6'7" height and 325-pound frame, meant curtains when he locked in on a frontal bear hug. Lifting shorter opponents off the ground, and with dangling feet and a face obviously in the worst pain ever, they quickly submitted.

There were times, depending on how villainous the opposition was, when he brought out a new weapon in his arsenal.

With those size 14 boots Hogan had given him, Jim would throw his foot into the face of a hard charging villain that immediately stopped him in his tracks. From there the bear hug was easy.

That first night in the Garden, Sgt. Goulet got the entire package. And so did the 19,000 at ringside, including Andy Warhol, Danny Devito and Joe Piscopo.

Jim, remembering the little things he had learned along the way, was able to stay in control and within himself, especially the breathing technique Dale Mann had taught him back in Bowling Green. "I never let the excitement get to me," says Jim. "It seemed like the bigger the moment, the calmer I was. Warhol came back in the dressing room after the match," Jim said. "He couldn't believe what he had just seen. He was shaking."

Anyone who saw the superstars in McMahon's stable came away impressed. Just on appearance alone the WWF was all about size… super size.

"Professional wrestling at this level was 100% visual," says Jim. "From the physical size to the antics in the ring. McMahon didn't want performers who looked like the guy next door, he wanted guys that people stopped and looked at."

And in the ring all of the moves, from the smacks to the face, the slaps to the chest, to the bombs-away drop kicks, they had to be done so the screaming fans in the far reaches of the arena could see them as if they were sitting on the front row.

"When you throw little bitty punches it's nothing," said Jim. "You've got to reach down and throw it from way down in Mississippi where everyone can see it. We didn't want anyone to miss a thing. Those little rabbit punches can't be seen, but those big round-house ones sure could. That's why over the years those intercollegiate wrestlers had to learn professional wrestling. Their moves had been quick and explosive, not easily seen. Kurt Angle was the exception.

"The things people think are phony are the things that are real. The punches don't hurt, but some of those chops and forearms sure did. One of the most believable moves is the pile driver where you get the opponent upside down and drive his head and neck into the mat. It's really not that dangerous if done right."

Wrestling had been a good-'ole-boy thing…especially in the South. If you knew somebody, there's a chance you could find yourself in a small time wrestling match. Often, brothers, cousins, or good friends could hook up with a local promoter and soon be a wrestler, albeit not a very good one.

"I never wanted anybody I knew, especially my family, in the business," says Jim. "Most of the time from the ones I knew who did it didn't turn out good for the family."

Vince McMahon changed professional wrestling more than any person ever.

Gorgeous George took the sport from carnival sideshows to black and white television. Jerry Lawler took it to small town gyms. Hulk Hogan took it to major arenas and stadiums. But McMahon took it to Madison Avenue and turned a night-out-with-the boys into an evening with the family.

He made wrestling the sport to watch and the place to be seen. He was all about bigger, and over time he created a billion dollar industry that he drug out of the closet and into the living room.

Jim Morris was right in the middle of it all. He was a part of McMahon's entertainment factory. Jim, like the others, had a story to tell, not necessarily a true one, but instead a story line that had been developed pertaining to his Kentucky heritage.

In addition to being physically imposing, the McMahon A-team had to have a stage presence that required them to not only talk in front of thousands, but to act.

Jim was more than a modern day grappler. He had to look good, talk good, possess star power, and ultimately be very entertaining.

Jim's proof of his star status was his inclusion in Hulk Hogan and Friends weekly television Saturday morning cartoon show that was aimed at bringing in young kids. Then came a Milton Bradley wrestling board game, followed by a Hillbilly Jim action doll. His image appeared on T-shirts, TV and newspaper ads, and various scripts for cameo appearances on primetime television shows. If it was good, Jim Morris was involved.

"I always tried promoting myself with a clean image," he said. "I stayed away from all of the bad stuff, which is why I enjoyed doing things that involve kids."

Jim found out how really big this wrestling stuff could be when he was doing a show at Notre Dame University.

"Pat Patterson came in where I was and said he had some legal papers for me from the WWF. I was a little concerned, but when he handed it to me it was a royalty check for all the stuff they had sold with my image. I couldn't believe it…$86,710.10."

Hillbilly Jim was all of that.

"The party was going on when I got there and I joined it," he says in referring to the WWF. "Most of the people you wouldn't want as friends, however, there were others that became really close friends. Some of those guys were the worst, not sure I even wanted to breath the same air…drug addicts and alcoholics.

"Chief Strongbow told me in the beginning 'these guys in wrestling will steal the dimes off your eyes and your friends aren't here…they're back home.'"

As Jim began to evolve in the WWF he never forgot the little lessons he learned along the way, and the advice he had been given by those he encountered.

He realized how lucky he was. Not having to spend years tolling in third rate venues, but instead seemingly catching a break by connecting with someone who knew someone who also knew someone.

Jim, by no means looked like the average guy, and that helped him open doors.

It had been Dirty Rhodes, back in Memphis, who educated him about all of the "snakes in the grass." He soon realized how many wrestlers were paranoid, trusting no one, especially promoters who cared only about themselves.

"Most of the guys in the early years were good to me because of my personality," says Jim, perhaps forgetting for a moment it was this trait that helped him survive growing up in the Bryant Village housing community in Bowling Green until he got big enough to kick ass.

There was David Schultz, known as Dr. Death who Jim says, "Many didn't like, but I did."

Schultz had a reputation, and from his actions he had earned it. He actually received more notoriety for his actions out of the ring than in it.

By now professional wrestling was rising above the smoke of small town wrestling. But the sport took a hit as to its legitimacy when in 1984, wrestlers Eddie Mansfield and Jim Wilson, spilled their guts on television's 20/20 about the state of affairs of wrestling.

As a follow-up, nothing hit home more than the blow to the side of the face 20/20 host John Stossel endured on camera from Schultz.

It was in late December 1984, back stage in Madison Square Garden with cameras rolling, Stossel looked at Schultz and told him his sport was fake. Dr. Death appeared agitated from the outset, and out of nowhere fired a hard open hand slap to Stossel's face.

"Was that fake," Schultz screamed at the stunned Stossel. "And that was just with my open hand."

But Schultz wasn't finished. Quickly he delivered another slap, knocking the television host to the floor. A second camera caught Stossel and his camera man quickly leaving the area.

It was not a flattering time for the WWF.

Schultz said he had been told by the WWF to hit Stossel during the interview segment, but it was denied. However, the WWF settled a Stossel lawsuit for $425,000.00.

The 20/20 reports, combined with an effort of a New York State senator from the Bronx to ban professional wrestling in the state, was thought to be a big blow to the sport. However, just three days after the Stossel interview with Schultz, 19,000 fans, the largest crowd in New Jersey wrestling history, showed up at the Meadowlands to see an event. The following month Madison Square Garden sold out two separate cards, one of which was part of a worldwide closed-circuit showing.

"Adrian Adonis, many thought, was a jerk," Jim said. "His real name was Ken Franks, and I remember in Flint, Michigan, at a show he got into it with a big old boy who had played defensive end at Georgia, named Danny Spivey. Spivey was about 6'6", 280 lbs., and he had literally knocked Adonis out cold and left him in the ring. Spivey came on back to the dressing room and Adonis came running in mad as hell. Spivey took a big left swing and hit him like a melon rind. Junkyard Dog and Pat Patterson were there too, and JYD told Pat to "let 'em fight." "I was on the card that night with Iron Mike Sharp and we were both there. Some of the best fights were in the dressing room. That night Adonis probably got what was coming to him, because he had a reputation of taking advantage of the young guys in the business."

Mr. Wonderful Paul Orendorff, was another big star in the WWF stable. With a body builder's physique and good looks he had no problem being a "heel" for most of his years in the sport.

"He was one of them who didn't like the fans," Jim says. "We'd be going through an airport and people would ask for autographs and he would go off on them. They called the fans marks, and would say, 'aw, the roar of the popcorn and smell of the fans.' It was a carnival thing that started back in the '20s and '30s."

Jim says, unfortunately, many of the wrestlers started believing their own gimmicks, in and out of the ring.

"Ric Flair got caught up in all of his hype, but over the years he was good to me," says Jim. "I had enough sense to listen to veterans like him and Harley Race. They were heels in the ring, but I learned a lot from them. I may not be a great dancer, but I'm a good follower."

It was in the dressing rooms throughout the country that so much of the businesses' education took place. Inside the ring is what the spectators in the arena saw, as well as millions of fans by way of television. But often the real competition was happening behind the scenes.

The WWF organizers were continuously on guard to maintain the illusion of the shows storyline. The heels and the baby faces were not to be palsey-wowsey with each other outside the ring. It was the kayfabe of it all. Remember, Chief Strongbow wanted Hillbilly Jim to always be, well, Hillbilly Jim, even to the point of driving and old pick-up truck. He certainly didn't want anyone seeing him socializing with Bobby Heenan.

Nevertheless, in the twisting, winding corridors of those large arenas, there was a secure sanctuary, where the guys could get together to discuss their upcoming match with the opponent, maybe even rehearse the "spots", and by all means prepare to give the thousands of fans first class entertainment. And entertainment was what it was all about.

"The dressing rooms were happening places," Jim offered. "We had an area where we could come in, lots of time in vans that had picked us up at the hotel. We used the area to warm-up, exercise, play cards, and some even dipped a little Skoal. We played jokes on each other and sometimes there would be fights. You've got to remember, we had some guys that just didn't like each other."

Unbeknownst to the fans, it was their actions that sometimes dictated how long a match would last.

"Going in, we knew the time span we were to do our show," says Jim. "The real test for us as performers was how charged up we could get the fans. There were many times we had them at fever pitch well before we had expected to be, so we wanted to end it there and that's what we did."

Fans invested of themselves, especially when actually attending a match. Emotionally involved in the match and storyline, some of these fans would actually spit on the combatants as well as hurling quarters and batteries. It was not always a pretty picture.

Promoters would closely monitor fan reactions to certain wrestlers and often based their story lines on what they thought the fans wanted.

On occasion, one of the wrestlers would be described by the announcers as a "scientific wrestler." This usually meant he wasn't one of those off-the-top-rope guys, bouncing from one side of the ring to the other. His moves usually were quick, precise moves that resulted into a slick take down of his confused-looking opponent. The truth was scientific wrestling wasn't what the fans were there to see. After all, professional wrestling was a sport that could not be scientifically explained.

Often the crowds would be worked into a frenzy. Metal barricades usually surrounded the ring, creating a barrier between the fans and wrestlers. Of course, part of the show's entertainment revolved around the "heels" ability to incense them. Most often a well-placed microphone ended up in the "heels" hand at the end of the match, taunting, not only the "baby face" he had just destroyed, but the fans as well.

WWF security was always nearby. As behemoth as the grapplers were, there were still fans, men and women, who wanted to show how tough they were, by helping those fallen good guys as they administered their form of justice.

"It could get a little dangerous after some of the main events," said Jim. "There were times when fans would turn cars over as they left the arena with wrestlers in them. Sometime the only way we could get out was in an ambulance."

Chapter Eleven

*P*rofessional wrestling was a rough, rowdy business, and it was often very difficult to separate the good guys from the bad guys, so Jim proceeded with caution. Just as he portrayed his aw-shucks, down-home, maybe-not-the brightest character in the ring, he was anything but that.

In his own way Jim Morris was very calculating, keeping an eye out for all of those snakes he had been warned about. Of course there were things he didn't particularly like about the McMahon operation, but what the heck. For sure he knew it wasn't a perfect world outside of wrestling either. He had been given an opportunity to turn his God-given athletic skills into a very lucrative business, and by-damn he wasn't about to rock this boat.

James Henry Morris, called by some "the little preacher" while attending tent revivals with his brother Dwight and mother Opal back in Allen County as a young boy, was smart enough to know this gig couldn't last forever.

Not only was his huge physique a head-turner even by WWF standards, so was his personality and ability to talk. Vince McMahon's number two requirement, after size, was to be able to handle a microphone in front of 20,000 screaming fans. For those who had both, it turned into a payday. And Jim Morris did, indeed, have both. That's why in the mid to late '80s he was voted the WWF's most popular, behind only Hulk Hogan.

Though he was no longer spending hours upon hours in a cramped-up car driving from one dimly lit gym or armory to another, now Jim was spending hours in airports and cramped-up plane seats. He didn't complain. It was part of the job, and besides, what else would he rather be doing?

A travel agency out of Greenwich, Connecticut, handled his arrangements and without his black plastic covered pocket sized travel log, even knowing what city he was in would have been difficult.

It was a good thing the money was good.

In his early days with the WWF he wrestled 38 straight nights in 38 different cities before a day off…one day, then he was back at it again. He was a wrestling superstar in the making, and he was only doing what the others were, too.

One of his lighter loads was in March 1986: Saturday, March 1, Baltimore; Sunday, Toronto, Canada; Monday, Toronto; Tuesday, San Francisco; Wednesday, Sacramento; Thursday, Baton Rouge; Friday, New Orleans; Saturday, Cincinnati; Sunday, Detroit; Monday, Salisbury, Maryland; Tuesday, Poughkeepsie, New York; Wednesday, Strasburg, Pennsylvania; Thursday, Providence, Rhode Island; Friday, Pittsburgh; Saturday, Chicago; Sunday, Madison Square Garden. All of this, which was a typical schedule, was followed by six days off.

Most sports are somewhat seasonal, but not wrestling. It's there 52 weeks a year. Because of this, it's the travel that often takes more out of the wrestlers than the match itself.

It was those days off that Jim would head back to Bowling Green to visit with his mother and kids, and say hello to a few friends. It was here that he could hang out, play a little music on his favorite guitar, and well, just be Jim Morris.

He felt comfortable. No autograph seekers, but if they did he was always glad to oblige. By now Jim was a well known commodity in town. Almost everyone knew him as Hillbilly Jim.

There were still times when he was asked to appear at fund raising events.

"Jim Morris gave of his time to so many local events at no charge," offered long time Western Kentucky University and Bowling Green sportscaster Wes Strader. "He has always remained the good hearted person he is today."

Strader was involved in one of those fundraisers in the early '90s at Western's Ag Expo Center along with Warren County Sheriff Jerry "Peanut" Gaines.

"We had promoted a match between Hillbilly, the Sheriff and me," Strader recalled. "A pretty good crowd showed up, mostly to see what Jim had in store for us. We rehearsed a few things before we got in the ring. The finish was Jim was going to take our heads and crack them together. He told 'Peanut' to lean to the right and for me to lean to the right when he rammed our heads."

But here's where it got interesting.

"Oh, it was beautiful," Hillbilly Jim said. "When the lights were turned on neither one of them remembered a thing we had gone over. Both of them looked like deer in a headlight. They panicked."

Jim, proceeded to body slam the Sheriff, and then pick the much smaller Strader up above his head with an airplane spin move.

"Jim and I are good friends, but I was scared to death," Strader said years later. "I kept saying 'put me down, Jim, put me down Jim.' He had the meanest look I've ever seen on a man."

Finally, when Hillbilly picked both of them up and prepared to crack their heads, Sheriff Gaines had forgotten which way he was supposed to lean, right or left.

"Luckily, I leaned the right way," Gaines laughed.

Western Kentucky University, and Coach Paul Sanderford in particular, got his Lady Topper basketball program in on Hillbilly Jim's notoriety. On February 24, 1989, with the number two ranked Tennessee Lady Vols coming to Diddle Arena, Sanderford was layering in his promotions to leave nothing to chance. For the coach it was more than just the game stuff, it was about entertaining those who bought tickets.

That's why he brought Jim in to referee a wrestling match between Hilltopper mascot "Big Red" against a "Gruesome Gorilla." It was all a part of the show, and, of course Big Red ultimately had his hand raised by Hillbilly Jim.

On March 31, 1985, Vince McMahon launched WrestleMania I without really knowing for sure there would ever be a II, III, IV or beyond. But as only the WWF machine could do it, money was not an issue when it came to its kickoff.

The celebrity non-wrestlers truly made WrestleMania I a spectacle. First you begin with the most famous sports venue in the world, Madison Square Garden. Then you bring in the most famous athlete in the world, Muhammad Ali as the special referee. The ring announcer was New York Yankee manager Billy Martin, who himself had been known to mix it up with a few fisticuffs over the years. And then out of nowhere, in a quirky sort of way, the timekeeper is Liberace, who could rival Gorgeous George when it came to sequins. For sure it had to be the top shelf of WWF stars to come close to what McMahon had assembled as a supporting cast. And it was.

Hulk Hogan teamed with Mr. T ("The A Team" television series and Clubber Lang in the movie Rocky III) to take on "heels," Rowdy Roddy Piper and Paul "Mr. Wonderful" Orendorff. In the other featured match Andre The Giant butted heads with Big John Studd. Right smack in the middle of it all officiating in the ring with Ali was Pat Patterson, McMahon's chief lieutenant. He was there to make sure this premier event went as planned. And it did.

Many of the matches had sidebars to them, and in WrestleMania I the big draw was that Andre had vowed to body slam the 400-pound Studd or, and this was big, retire from wrestling forever. Studd then said if Andre was able to match his promise he would have to pay The Giant $15,000.

"The world of sports entertainment changed forever when WrestleMania began," Jim said. "Fans couldn't get enough of it. These guys were almost freaks when it came to size, and then when you mix in celebrities that everybody knew, it gave the sport legitimacy."

Missing from it all was Hillbilly Jim. "I would have been there if it hadn't been for my knee injury in San Diego," he said.

Vince McMahon, who hot-wired his father's passion for the promotional angle, would delve into wrestling's old days in order to explore what might still work today.

McMahon marveled at an Argentina wrestler named Antonio Rocca, who was the first to ever literally fly around the ring, slapping opponents in the face with his bare feet. He created moves called the airplane spin and flying head scissors.

"Other than Milton Berle (comedian), Rocca did more to sell TV sets than anyone else in the 1950s and early '60s," McMahon said.

Rocca's matches never left the ring. Little need for props such as tables, chairs, ladders or ringside brawls. His flying body was all he needed to take care of the likes of Dick the Bruiser, Nature Boy Buddy Rogers or Freddie Blassie who were well-known villains back in the day.

McMahon was always in search of talent, the bigger the better. But he also kept an eye out for that acrobatic performer, one who could win over the fans, and perhaps make up for a lack of size by flipping, whirling, and leaping as if on a trampoline in order to defeat a larger opponent. Any move that included the top rope was a good thing.

The WWF wanted it all.

Everybody was talking about wrasslin". From truck drivers to business execs, from housekeepers to their high salaried employers, they now had a common subject to talk about.

In real life he was Terry Bollea, but when he became Hulk Hogan and hooked up with McMahon, the wrestling renaissance began. He may not have been the first Hulk of notoriety, but for sure he was smart enough to pull together a combination of two popular television shows and turn it into marketing genius.

Lou Ferrigno's Incredible Hulk and Hogan's Heroes had already done a number on family television audiences across America with good over evil, so when Terry Bollea turned on Hulkamania, it seemed like an entire nation was ready to follow. The Iron Sheik from Iran and Nikolai Volkoff from Russia didn't stand a chance against the 6'7" 300-pound Hulkster.

Wrasslin" leaped out of those darkened living rooms where many a grandmother kicked over a snuff can in her excitement of seeing her hero win. The family and neighbors all settled in around the black and white to see it all play out.

But then McMahon turned on every light in the house. No, he didn't reinvent anything. The formula was already there. It has always been the heels against the baby faces.

From the 1930s the business never really changed except for the promotions and cable TV.

Gorgeous George (George Raymond Wagner) didn't enter the ring with a sophisticated sound system playing the latest tunes or flashing lights of all colors criss-crossing the arena. But make no mistake, every move of his prancing entrance was planned to the nth degree.

The fans jeered George with disgust, even though they were there to only see him. His flashy gold robe with his name embossed across the back, complimented his permed blond curly hair. His arrogant strut brought the fans to fever pitch. And with the flip of his head, followed by pulling gold bobby pens and tossing them into the frenzied crowd, who leaped and dove to get their hands on one, he knew he was in control.

Further implementing the plan, the Gorgeous One would strut to each side of the ring to make sure everyone who had bought a ticket could see him. Still in no hurry to face his opponent, a valet, in slow motion, would help George out of his flowing robe, soon after spraying the ring with a perfume snifter.

The crowd, not realizing it, had been sucked in, just as the opponent that night had. The match had little to do with whoever the opposition was. It was all about the fizz, and when fans left the arena, they weren't talking about how great the match was, but instead how obnoxious Gorgeous George was.

For McMahon it was simple. He didn't have to think outside of the box at all. He just had to see what was already in the one he had.

The storylines were easy…just follow how the politicians did it. One party would love each other, then hate each other, only to love each other again. It would be part of the script that never went away.

Chapter Twelve

With Hillbilly Jim now entrenched in the WWF, the travel was the grind.

"When you consider we were only in the ring an average of 15 to 20 minutes a day, that left 23 hours we had to deal with," Jim says. "The WWF would give us all our travel tickets, and I've seen grown men cry because of their schedule. We've all cracked before, and just about everybody at one time or another has gone home.

"We had to pay our own expenses…food, hotels, car rentals and all. Then the WWF decided to arrange for rental cars that we were supposed to ride together in if the next show was drivable. But as you can guess, that didn't work out when some of the guys would get left behind."

It was almost humanly impossible to keep any sort of sanity in his life. He didn't begrudge the money, but the same couldn't be said about one period in his career when he performed 63 straight nights. Fifty-three of those days required air travel.

Along the way, in and out of world-class arenas and in and out of even more airports, Jim and his wrestling buddies would run into other celebrities, not necessarily wrestlers.

Often, Jim was more recognizable than the professional athletes or even movie stars. It was difficult not to notice the mammoth wrestlers strolling through an airport…even if you didn't know their names. But for Jim Morris his Hillbilly Jim character was not easy to miss.

"We'd see George Brett (Kansas City Royal baseball star) here and there," Jim recalled. "He was a jerk to kids wanting his autograph. He gave baseball players a bad name as far as I was concerned. All they (baseball players) do is stand around scratching themselves. I'll be honest, when I saw the way he treated people I was looking for a confrontation with him."

There was another encounter he had, this one with a movie star.

"Loretta Swit (MASH) was not friendly at all," he laughed. "That made me want to needle her some, so I put my arm over her shoulder for a quick photo. She had to smile, but was not very happy about it. We had been on the Regis Philbin Show."

It always seemed that Jim knew someone who knew someone and when all of the dots were connected everyone knew everyone. With Jim's easy-going personality it was easy to see why many gravitated his way.

Jim's friend, Bruce Swayze, hooked him up with super promoter Buddy Lee, who held a portfolio full of A and B tiered celebrities. Among the A list were Chubby Checker, George Jones, Johnny Rivers, John Conlee, Waylon Jennings, Jerry Lee Lewis, Willie Nelson, Bill Monroe and Ray Charles.

"I met Buddy, who was behind the promotion for Farm Aid," says Jim. "He began to book me for personal appearances and advertising spots for different kinds of business."

With introductions to the likes of Bill Monroe and Willie Nelson, Jim was now on his way to becoming involved into what was really his first love—music.

He was a natural fit to be a part of the Farm Aid event in Austin, Texas on July 4, 1986.

"Growing up where I did in Barren, Allen, and Warren County, being around farming was ingrained in me," Jim said at the time.

Buddy Lee thought Hillbilly Jim would also be a good fit for the popular television show Hee Haw. After all, most of the cast, men and women, were already wearing bib overalls, so Jim would hit the ground running and easily be able to stay in his WWF character.

It helped that Lee had been a wrestler himself years before, even marrying one of the greatest women grapplers of all-time.

"He married the Fabulous Moolah," Jim said. "She was so good and well respected that the girls she beat up in the ring would apologize to her. Now that was something."

Jim continued:

"Buddy sounded like Marlon Brando in 'The Godfather' when he talked," says Jim. "And he knew everybody. It was actually Steve Popovich, Sr., Buddy went through to make the Hee Haw deal."

Popovich, Sr., had worked with Epic Records, and represented Boz Skaggs and Meat Loaf among some of his clients, so he recognized that agent Buddy Lee's association with Hillbilly Jim made a lot of sense for a Hee Haw connection.

In the ring Jim wore Oshkosh overalls, but for Hee Haw his contract called for him to wear the Liberty brand. Some of Jim's promotional pictures showed him wearing a Toughskin overalls label, made by Sears.

"They had to make mine special," he said of the Liberty overalls. "They measured me, and I was close to getting an endorsement from them, but they already had a contract with George Lindsey (Goober)."

Jim said that the Hee Haw program was filmed in Nashville twice a year, one time for the comedy segments and the other for the musical acts.

In his career Jim went through 10 to 15 pairs of overalls. "They're more durable than you think," he says. "The straps would sometime break or get ripped off, so I retired them."

The Popovich relationship didn't just end with Steve, Sr. Years later Jim would become associated with Steve, Jr., on a Sirius Radio Show out of Nashville.

Jim would do a lot of his out-of-the-ring interviews tongue-in-cheek. He was a natural, playing his character to the hilt. Talking in front of crowds never bothered him. It has been said that one of man's biggest fears is standing up and speaking to a crowd, but Jim had overcome that years ago.

"Shucks, I was used to it from the time I'd get up and do a little preachin' and testifying at those tent revivals with mama and Dwight back in Allen County when I was eight or nine."

In March 1986 in an interview with the *Toronto Sun*, with a wink of the eye he proved that he was indeed just a hick from Mudlick…just a dumb country boy.

"My mama is proud of me," he told the newspaper. "I always knew I was gonna be different. I always knew I was gonna do something different with my life…I just felt that I gotta do something weird. I can't handle a 9 to 5 job."

It was easy to read between the lines that the *Sun*'s reporter wasn't completely buying into Jim's alter ego. He was quick to catch on to his deadly sense of humor, while noting that Jim's IQ must be close to his fighting weight of 305.

"I could be the mayor of Mudlick if I wanted to be," he told the writer. "But you shouldn't write that. I'm just a country boy."

Years later in 1999, after Jim had been away from the ring for several years, Keith Lawrence of the Owensboro, Kentucky *Messenger-Inquirer* picked up on the continued popularity of Hillbilly Jim.

Perhaps, Lawrence wrote, Hillbilly ought to think about running for Governor or maybe even Congress. After all, it wouldn't be the first time a wrestler had been elected to public office. Jesse "The Body" Ventura had run a straight-shooter campaign in becoming Governor of Minnesota. Bob Backlund was elected to Congress out of Connecticut, and Jerry Lawler in a love-hate relationship had run for mayor of Memphis.

The Owensboro writer set out to create a Lum and Abner type dialogue between some of the locals at a cafe.

The dialog went like this:

"Shoot, he's from down around Bowling Green," said one. "We oughta run him," said the other. "I'd vote for him fer durn near anything," said another. "He's a good ole boy, and we ain't got enough good ole boys left."

The WWF, too, recognized there weren't all that many good ole boys around. That's why when Jim suffered the knee injury they quickly came up with the Cousin Junior and Uncle Elmer thing. They were really never in the same league with the Hillbilly. It was difficult to create a good natured lovable character when it didn't come naturally. That was always the difference. Jim Morris and Hillbilly Jim shared much more than incredible athletic skills and a Delta Force work ethic. They were both good people.

"Remember, in my entire wrestling career I was never a heel (bad guy)," Jim says. "So I never had to get out of character when it came to being nice to my fans. Remember, I was just a hillbilly who tried to help someone who was being taken advantage of (Hulk Hogan). I was never to appear to be over accomplished…always scuffling until someone pissed me off."

As Hillbilly Jim, he also took his nicety's to an almost unheard of level in professional wrestling. He would shake hands with his villainous opponent even when he lost.

"It was my style, my character," he says. "I could have sulked and stomped and shook the ropes like a sore looser. But instead, I do an aw shucks pose, slap my hands together with an 'I'll get him next time' attitude. Why not? That is really who I am and the fans loved it. Win or lose, I'd dance around the ring with a big smile to the song 'Don't Go Messin' With a Country Boy.'"

Jim won even when he lost, and by the mid-'80s he was a WWF Super Star.

His rise was relatively quick. For one thing people took notice of him in and out of the ring. There were others who were just as tall, even though his abundance of hair gave him the appearance well above his 6-7 height. What made the difference was his 64-inch chest, and his ability to speak in front of large crowds.

"TV time was precious," he said. "The more exposure, the more popular, and then the more money you made. The more corny...the better."

Corny was good in the golden days of the WWF. Jim's take on it now is that the ad-lib, off-the-wall dialogue of his days in the ring are gone. The feeder grounds, Jim says, have been destroyed.

"We did our promos ourselves in the ring," he adds. "We were trusted to say the right things to get the fans riled up. Now, in this day and time, they have writers who create and script what is said.

"It's million dollar performers with 10-K brains now days...no charisma today. You've got to connect with the people...these young kids wrestling today don't, and the fans can tell."

One of those who really connected with the fans in the mid-'80s was Roderick George Toombs, a Canadian who went by the wrestling name of Rowdy Roddy Piper. The mere mention of his name could set off a crowd of Hulk Hogan's or Hillbilly Jim fans.

Piper was the best there was with a microphone close to his mouth. McMahon knew what he was doing when he signed the undersized, kilt-wearing Piper. He was a wordsmith when it came to crude, insulting comments that often questioned another wrestler's heritage or lack of brains on his TV segment called Piper's Pit.

"He was a big star before McMahon got him," says Jim Morris. "His wit was better than his wrestling. He was magic with the microphone."

To prove Jim's point, the Rowdy one used his ability to disrupt, antagonize, and ad-lib to become one of wrestling's biggest stars, headlining some of the WWF's biggest matches. One of those was the biggest. Piper teamed with Paul Orendorff in Wrestle Mania I where they were defeated by Hogan and Mr. T on March 31, 1985, in Madison Square Garden.

Piper knew what he was doing in and out of the ring, Jim added. He was not one of those who tried to hurt you in the ring like a few others did.

On July 31, 2015, Piper who coined one of the all-time famous lines of, "Just when you think you have all the answers, I change the questions," died at the age of 61.

Jim recovering back home with his coon hounds.

Muhammad Ali was the referee of record in WrestleMania.

Fans welcome Jim back from his knee injury in 1985.

Jim is in the studio at the Hit Factory in New York City with music producer Joel Dorn as they record "Don't Go Messin With A Country Boy" in 1986.

Liberace with Captain Lou Albano at WrestleMania

Paul "Mr. Wonderful" Orendorff

New York Yankees manager Billy Martin

Jesse "The Body" Ventura

New York City mayor Ed Koch and Jim arm wrestle at a fundraiser wheelchair basketball game. "He is pretty strong for a city boy," Jim said of the mayor.

Jim and his cousin Vicky Hindman in 1986.

Hulk Hogan, Cyndi Lauper, and Captain Lou Albano

Jim works out in 1986 at Vince Girondo's famous gym in Los Angeles.

Jim and Dallas Cowboy defensive end Harvey Martin at WrestleMania II in 1987.

Wrestlers Danny Spivey and Jim with Atlanta Falcons Bill Fralic before Wrestle-Mania II, WWF vs. NFL, in 1987.

It was the Rasslers against the NFL in the Pontiac Silverdome in WrestleMania II in 1987. That's Jim to the left with Iron Sheik grabbing his neck.

Baseball celebrity Bob Uecker with Jim at WrestleMania in 1987.

Jim and Chicago Bears Hall of Famer Dick Butkus on the set in Los Angeles, filming a national Chevy pickup commercial in 1987.

Jim with Mr. T and Hulk Hogan

Jim laughes it up at a WWF event with (l-r) Ken Patera, Junkyard Dog, and Outback Jack.

Jim waves to the crowd at Farm Aid in 1987.

Country singer John Anderson and Jim at Farm Aid.

Country singer Johnny Paycheck at Farm Aid in Austin, Texas in 1987.

Jim with the late Owen Hart and his wife Martha in 1987.

January 15, 1988

Hillbilly Jim
c/o Jim Morris
1054 South Cooper
Memphis, TN 38104

Dear Jim:

Thank you for being a part of HEE HAW once again. It was great having you back on the show.

Your guest appearances will be on the following shows:

AIR DATE	SHOW #	REPEAT AIR DATE
87485	2/6/88	7/16/88
87490	4/30/88	8/20/88

Enclosed please find photos taken on the set during taping.

Come back and see us real soon. It was a pleasure working with you again. Have a healthy and successful '88.

Sincerely,

Sam Lovullo
Producer

SL:kbj
Enclosure

cc: Mike Webber

ORD PROGRAM SERVICES, INC.
40710, Nashville, Tennessee 37214
(615) 889-6840

George "Goober" Lindsey with Jim on the Hee Haw set.

Linda Thompson with Jim on Hee Haw. Linda is the former girlfriend of Elvis, and her two children are by ex-husband Bruce Jenner.

Country music star Del Reeves and Jim at the Hee Haw taping at the Grand Ole Opry.

Pictured l-r: Mike Rotunda, Jim, Hulk Hogan, and Barry Windham flank NBC reporter Bob Costas during a "Sports World" special.

Wrestling legend Nick Bockwinkle with Jim and Stu Hart.

Loretta Swit with Jim on the Regis Show.

Jim on the set of the Regis Philbin Show in New York City in 1988.

Jim and his mother Opal just before Wrestle-Mania II in Chicago.

Jim and Vince McMahon in Baltimore in 1986.

Jim with B. Brian Blair in Miami in 1987.

The Ultimate Warrior and his wife with Jim in Salt Lake City, Utah, in 1988.

Jim tangles with Big John Studd in 1989 in Providence, Rhode Island.

Hacksaw Jim Duggan and Ken Patera with Jim in 1988.

Arnold Skoland stands between Mr. Fuji and Jim before their "tuxedo match" in Madison Square Garden in 1988.

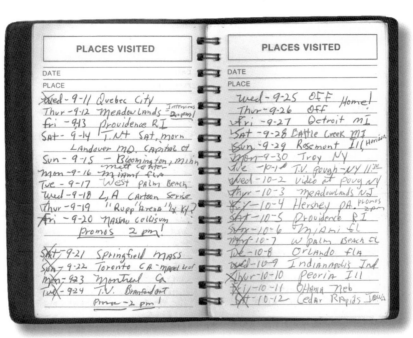

Samples from Jim's Travel Log.

Jim stands between The British Bulldogs in 1986 at Madison Square Garden.

Jim hams it up with Barry Windham (l) and Mike Rotunda at the Nassau Coliseum in 1986.

Jim with Jumpin Jimmy Brunzell in Toronto, Canada in 1988.

Billy Jack Haynes and Jim in 1989 at Hershey Park Arena.

Jim and Iron Mike Sharp in New Orleans in 1989.

Jim picks guitar with friends Tim Ford seated with Steve Ford at his mom's house in 1990.

WORLD WRESTLING FEDERATION

1055 Summer Street
Post Office Box 3857
Stamford, CT 06905
203 352 8600
FAX: 203 352 8699
TELEX: 643283 TITAN STM

Writer's direct line: 203 352

November 17, 1986

Mr. Jim Morris
Jim Morris Enterprises Inc.
1054 South Cooper
Memphis, TN 38104

Dear Mr. Morris:

The enclosed report details the royalties due to you for the period 4/1/86 through 7/1/86 and includes all mail order and venue merchandise sales as well as all licensee, video, dolls and other toys sold and reported to us for the period.

The following is a summary of this royalty payment:

Dolls & Toys (LJN)	$62,050.43
Video Cassettes (VHS)	4,878.62
Licensees & Concessions	103.25
Total Royalties	$67,032.30

If you have any questions, please call either Teri Mella or myself at our office.

Yours truly,

Douglas G. Sages
Senior Vice President – Finance

DGS:lmf

cc: L. E. McMahon
     V. K. McMahon

Letter from WWF, November 17, 1986.

(L-r) Jim with Mike Hagan, brother Dwight and Tommy Hagan, on Christmas 1992.

Dear Hillbilly Jim,

My name is Michael Kopel and I'm 15 years old. I am a real big fan of yours and you are my favorite wrestler in the world. I've seen almost all your matches. I saw you fight Big John Studd at the Nassau Coliseum a while ago and that was one of the greatest matches I ever saw. Can you please send me an autographed picture of yourself to hang up on my wall. Thank You very much. Also, if its not too much trouble can you please send one for my sister Stephanie. Thanks again.

Your #1 fan,
Michael Kopel

My address is: **30 Hallock Meadow Dr. No.
Stony Brook, NY 11790**

Letter from fan (Stony Brook, New York).

Martha Brown Middle School

Neil E. Petty, Principal   •   Margaret M. Van Haneghan, Assistant Principal

September 20, 1990

World Wrestling Federation
1055 Summer Street
P.O. Box 3857
Stamford, Connecticut 06905

Att: Hillbilly Jim

Dear Jim:

With much gratitude, we at the Martha Brown Middle School are so very appreciative of your experience with us on Monday, September 17. Your visit kicked off a wonderful beginning for students and staff. It mobilized the entire student body to get involved and participate. Students made posters, wrote poems, raps and every child and teacher made their own gold horseshoe. As you know, we will be publishing a book based on what students wrote on their gold horseshoe. We will send you a copy as soon as we receive it.

Jim, I also would like to comment on your talk to the student body. It was very powerful to have someone of your public stature share your thoughts and philosophy of life. Your message of trusting your-self and choosing to follow your moral standards was well received. You are to be commended for your personal commitment to investing in the youth of America.

Sincerely,

Vita Waite

Vita Waite and the Entire Staff of
Martha Brown Middle School

VW/gc

Letter from Martha Brown School, September 20, 1990.

VIA FEDERAL EXPRESS

**WORLD
WRESTLING
FEDERATION®**

1055 Summer Street
Post Office Box 3857
Stamford, CT 06905
203 352 8600
FAX: 203 352 8699
TELEX: 643283 TITAN STM

October 31, 1990

Mr. Jim Morris
1524 Virginia Avenues Place
Bowling Green, KY 42101

Dear Jim:

I'd like to invite you to join me for the American
Sportscasters Hall of Fame Awards Dinner on Thursday,
November 29 at the Marriott Marquis in Manhattan. I am
enclosing a copy of the invitation for this gala which
you may refer to for the specifics. Titan Sports will be
taking three tables which will be filled with a mixture
of office talent, announcing talent and wrestling talent!

Please let Emily know as soon as possible if you will be
free to attend. I would like to cover your expenses to
come to town and attend this event. Since this is a
black tie event, if you need to rent a tuxedo I'll be
glad to cover that expense as well.

Please contact TCA to make your travel arrangements if
you can make it.

Looking forward to seeing you there!

Best,

Vincent K. McMahon

VKM/ef

Letter from Vince McMahon, October 31, 1990.

TO: Hillbilly Jim   CC: S. AGNONE
                                    T. BUCHANAN
FROM: Licia Murphy   M. CARLUCCI
                                    J.J. DILLON
DATE: February 6, 1991   T. EMANUEL
                                    T. GARVIN
RE: Personal Appearance   D. GLOVER
        Toy Fair   V. MCMAHON
        New York City   P. PATTERSON
        Monday, February 11, 1991   S. PLANAMENTA
        5:30PM to 8:00PM   I. RICE
                                    C. ROZMUS
                                    S. TAYLOR

WORLD WRESTLING FEDERATION
1055 Summer Street
Post Office Box 3857
Stamford, CT 06905
203 352 8600
FAX: 203 352 8699
TELEX: 643283 TITAN STM

Below please find your itinerary for your appearance at
the Toy Fair Party in New York City on Monday, February
11, 1991 from 5:30PM to 8:00PM.

Ilene Rice and myself will be at the appearance with
you.

MONDAY, FEBRUARY 11, 1991

You will be picked up by limousine at the Travelodge on
10th Avenue at 4:45PM and taken directly to the
appearance.

APPEARANCE: 5:30PM TO 8:00PM
TOY FAIR
THE TOY BUILDING
200 FIFTH AVENUE CLUB
NEW YORK, N.Y.
CONTACT: Serg Gjolanga (212) 675-2080

Directly following the appearance you will be taken
back to the Stamford Sheraton Hotel, in the WWF van, by
Tony Z. Gene Okerlund, Bobby Heenan and Andre will be
riding back to Connecticut with you.

If you have any questions, please feel free to call me
at (203) 353-2873 or at home at (203) 834-9898.

Regards,
Licia

Letter from WWF, February 6, 1991.

Jim and Cousin Luke (Gene Lewis) discuss what is next.

Singer Little Richard and Jim in New York City in the late 1980s.

Hulk Hogan and Jim.

Jim talks to a group of kids in Glasgow, Kentucky in 1993.

Following Jim's active career, he "man-aged" the Godwins to a tag team title.

Coliseum Video promotion

Jim and The Godwins celebrate after a win.

Jim advertising for Piggy's Pizza in Boston, Massachusetts.

Jim and Robin Leech, host of Lifestyles of the Rich & Famous, 1991.

Hulk Hogan's Rock 'N' Wrestling cartoon promotion.

Actor Charlton Heston with Jim.

Actor John Voight with Jim.

Jim proudly holds his two symbolic gold Epic record albums for "The Wrestling Album" in 1986 and "Piledriver" in 1987.

Jim performs on stage at the House of Blues in Los Angeles in 1994.

Jim in front of Big Ben in London.

Jim with ZZ Top at his Sirius radio show in Nashville in 2006.

Jim with Coach Don Webb at his retirement party at Bowling Green High.

Jim at a reunion of some of Coach Webb's players.

Jim with high school Coach Don Webb and former teammate Frank Ragland.

Jim with former Purple teammate Steve Carter and Lloyd Campbell.

Bruce Swayze with wife Bonnie and Jim.

Jim and country singer Charlie Pride

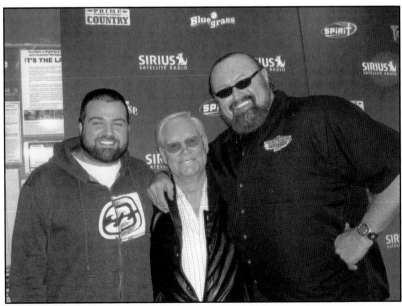

Sirius radio producer Steve Popovich Jr. and Jim with country singer George Jones.

Jim stands between music producer Cowboy Jack and songwriter John Prine.

Coliseum Video owner Arthur Morowitz and Jim at a vendor show.

Hulk Hogan, Koko B. Ware and Jim at a WWF event.

Jim with Hall of Famer, Jimmy "Mouth of the South" Hart in Dallas in 2001.

Jim with The Kentucky Headhunters at a show in Nashville.

Jim with Jim on a South Carolina bus tour in 2006.

Sirius Radio promo poster for Jim's radio show.

Jim and Steve Ford pose for a cover shoot of their Hoo Doo Men c.d.

Jim with NHL hockey great Gordie Howe, Bruce Swayze and Clarence Clemmons on the ice.

Jim and Jerry "The King" Lawler on a Fan Axess Tour in Memphis in 2006.

Jim with his favorite blues guitar player Chris Cain at an appearance in St. Louis in 2006.

(L-R) Legends The Fabulous Moolah, Jim, Mae Young, Bobby Heenan, and Lord Alfred Hayes.

Jim and wrestler Tug Boat

Jim presents Kentucky Colonel commission to wrestling great Stone Cold Steve
Austin.

Jim performing at a country music show at Disneyland in California in 1996.

Jim with Mean Gene Okerlund and Jimmy Hart.

Jim stands between brothers Johnny Valiant and "Handsome" Jimmy Valiant.

Jim with legend Glen Campbell.   *Jim with singer Johnny Rivers.*

Wrestler "Million Dollar Man" Ted DiBiase.

"The American Dream" Dusty Rhodes and Jim.

Jim with Motorhead lead singer Lemmy in Houston during WrestleMania.

Jim with singer-songwriter John Fogerty.

Jim with singer Ray Stevens.

George "The Animal" Steele and Jim stand on each side of a fan at WrestleMania in New York.

Jim and wrestler Big Vadar "pose-it-up" at a convention.

On a visit to the U.S. Mint, Jim holds $1.2 million in $100,000 bills. Note President Woodrow Wilson's picture on the bills.

(L-R) Chris Nowinski, Jimmy Hart, Roddy Piper with Jim at a WWF event.

Jim with one of his closest friends in the video business, Gary Ongst from London, Ky.

Jim and Jake "The Snake" Roberts

Jim with entertainer Charlie Daniels.

In the ring at a fund raising event in Bowling Green in the 1990s, Jim is surrounded by Warren County Sheriff Jerry "Peanut" Gaines, sportscaster Wes Strader, and wrestling mentor Bruce Swayze.

Jim perfoming with an orchestra at the Chicago Pier during a video trade show.

Jim guitars it up in the studio during a Sirius radio show.

Jim and legendary guitar player Duane Eddy.

Jim and wrestler Honky Tonk Man in Las Vegas.

Jim and wrestler Superstar Billy Graham, whose real name is Wayne Coleman.

Wrestler Terry Funk and Jim

Jim and Leapin Lanny Poffo, brother of Macho Man Randy Savage.

Jim and Ric Flair at a WWF event.

L-R: DJs Alamo Jones, Cowboy Jack, and Marshall Chapman, who wrote "Don't Go Messin with a Country Boy," next to Jim.

Jim stands between the Iron Sheik and Nikolai Volkoff.

(L-R) Wrestlers Terry Taylor, Bruno Sammartino, Jim, and Larry Zbyszko.

Chief Jay Strongbow (Joe Scarpa) and Jim. It was Chief who helped with Hillbilly Jim's wrestling name.

Jim laughs it up with former NFL star and actor Fred "The Hammer" Williamson at a trade show in Philadelphia in 1992.

Jim and wrestler Bret Hart

Jim and The Rock at WrestleMania 17 in Houston.

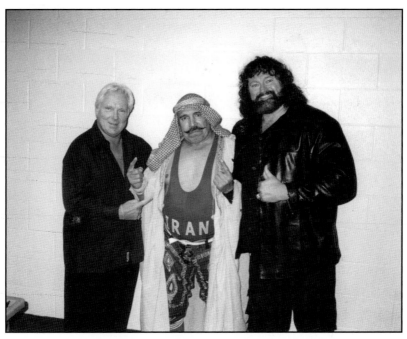

Jim with Bobby "The Brain" Heenan and The Iron Sheik at WrestleMania 17.

Jim and Earth Quake (John Tenta) at WrestleMania 17.

Jim stands between Rowdy Roddy Piper and Red Bastine in Dallas in 2001.

Dusty Rhodes and Jim in Stanford, Connecticut in 2006.

Jim with Classy Freddie Blassie at Hall of Fame induction in New York City in 1997.

Jim plays with good friend Kenny Lee and Rico Thomas in one of their many performances together.

Jim and wrestler Owen Hart.   *Jimmy Hart and Jim at a WWE event.*

Marty Applebaum and Jim stand behind Coliseum Video owner Arthur Morow-itz.

Jim with music associates (L-R) Steven Van Zant, Steve Popovich Jr., and legends Cowboy Jack and D.J. Alamo Jones.

(L-R) Albert Bailey, Tim Ford, Luby Chumbul, Jim, and Bob Sanborn.

Jim with his physical therapist, Paul Gray of Bowling Green, Ky.

Jim with the 1987 Lincoln he bought for his mother; he still drives it today!

Jim, in 2016, stands in front of the first house he lived in when he, his mother and brother Dwight moved to Bowling Green from Allen County.

Jim on front of his former home in Bryant Village in Bowling Green.

Jim serenades with Christmas songs at the home of Gary and Deborah West in 2014.

Writer Gary West stands between Jim and Kenny Davis, who was captain of the 1972 U.S. Olympic bastketball team.

Jim and Deborah West in 2014.

Chapter Thirteen

Vince McMahon, Jr., had his ear to the ground when it came to almost every aspect of marketing. Merchandising clothing, action figures and pay-for-view were genius. But perhaps none was more effective than when his WWF introduced "Rock 'n' Wrestling."

"It started when I came in the business," says Jim. "And it was as big as anything that had been done in the entertainment business."

What McMahon did was take MTV star Cyndi Lauper and weave her star power into his heel versus baby face story lines, thus putting professional wrestling on another tier, which meant millions of more fans and zillions of more dollars.

A few of the veteran wrestlers weren't ready to buy into this new music thing. They didn't really understand the marketing-entertainment aspect and the direction McMahon was headed. Though they were good inside the ring where it was heels and baby faces, how would professional wrestling be with, of all things, these same grapplers singing together on a wrestling album? Before, not able to be seen eating together or even traveling together, would the mystique no longer be there?

But most of all would the fans still believe? It's funny how sometimes life gets in the way…and now Jim would soon be getting back to his roots of music combined with his money making wrestling career. Yes, his life was good.

—⟋⟍—

Hello, "Rock 'n' Wrestling." Could professional wrestling and music co-exist? We were about to find out.

MTV and singing sensation Cyndi Lauper had been persuaded to become involved with the WWF at the insistence of her then manager and boyfriend David Wolff.

Wolff was one of those crazy-thinkers, always looking to expand Lauper's fan base by going to extremes other than just her pink-colored hair. He had been a wrestling fan from the Bruno Sammartino and Haystacks Calhoun days, and now with Cyndi Lauper he saw much more than large men, slugging and throwing each other around in local gyms and VFW halls. He saw the soap opera that could result from confrontation between a heel and a baby face. It would be the high-energy of the WWF mixed with the high powered music he would help generate. He knew the mix would work.

"It wasn't hard to convince Cyndi," Wolff said. "We wanted to get Captain Lou Albano involved. She had met him a couple of years earlier on a plane. I told her to roll with me on this. She has an amazing sense of humor, even though she wasn't really sure where all of this was going."

Although Wolff had this idea, in order to get it moving he had to get McMahon's approval to use Albano.

Through a friend, Wolff got a meeting set up with the McMahons and convinced the WWF czar the combination of Cyndi Lauper and professional wrestling would be good for both.

"The promotions we would do would take their soap opera lives into the real world," Wolff said. "I just let my imagination run wild. Vince and I traded ideas and we were ready to give it a go. The key was getting our story line outside of the wrestling community. MTV took it to the real world."

In order for Lauper to be introduced she had to become the "manager" of Wendi Richter, who was wrestling the Fabulous Moolah for the women's world WWF title. Naturally, Wendy won and Cyndi Lauper was in.

Lauper and Captain Lou became joined at the hip with the overweight wrestler playing the role of her father in the MTV video "Girls Just Wanna Have Fun" in 1983.

"MTV's highest rated videos were those that involved those WWF characters," Wolff said. "It brought the sport mainstream."

The "Girls" video was recognized by VH1, Rolling Stone, and MTV as the greatest music video of all-time.

To even think that Wolff and Lauper could create such a media stir with, of all things wrasslin', was beyond even the far-reaching ideas McMahon could present.

Cyndi Lauper had sold 50 million records, named to the Songwriters Hall of Fame, and been on the cover of *Time*, *Newsweek* and *People* magazines. And now she was teaming up with Lou Albano, a former University of Tennessee football player who walked around with rubber bands pierced into his face with safety pins, to help raise over $4 million for MS.

It was at a sold out Madison Square Garden with music legend Dick Clark in the middle of the ring honoring Lauper and Albano for their efforts to fight MS, that a funny thing happened on the way to a wrestling match.

With glass-front framed records being presented to the two, suddenly out of nowhere Rowdy Roddy Piper appeared in the ring and took control of the microphone. And wouldn't you know it, he grabbed the framed records, taking credit for the promotions success, and then smashed it over the head of Captain Lou. Bedlam reined.

Piper threw Lauper across the ring, and as David Wolff standing nearby, came to her aid...all 5-10, 138-pounds of him...Piper picked him up and slammed him into the ring's canvas.

"It was unlike anything I'd ever been involved in my life," Wolff says. "Everybody in the place, including security, had bought into it."

Of course, Wolff knew what was happening. He had orchestrated it all.

"I knew for sure I had to experience what being body slammed by Rowdy Roddy would be like before we ever did it in Madison Square Garden," he offered. "So Piper and I met up in Connecticut to rehearse it. He did it several times and I was still uneasy about it. When Piper jumped into the ring that night I was scared to death because I knew what was coming. It really did hurt and I had to see a chiropractor several times after it."

The sell-out crowd was stunned. It was so believable because here was a little skinny non-wrestler being body slammed by a WWF star.

"If he'd done that to another wrestler it wouldn't have had the realism it did with me," he added. "They carried me out on a stretcher and Madison Square Garden was in complete silence. It was so real. We laughed our asses off later."

Wolff added that he had the foresight to replace the real glass with "movie" glass in order to keep those in the ring from getting cut by flying glass.

It was the Cyndi Lauper/David Wolff involvement that helped launch WrestleMania as a pay-for-view event.

People were now watching wrestling that had never watched it before. The real world credibility of it all was beginning to gain traction. Some had viewed it as a subculture…but not any more.

Ultimately, Wolff always realizing Cyndi Lauper, at the end of the day was a recording artist, faded from the wrestling scene naturally, as the novelty of their sideshow began to wear off.

"We couldn't do any more," Wolff observed. "We went back to our music and wrestling continued to grow with the many new fans we had helped bring in."

In reality, Cyndi Lauper and professional wrestling did not need each other. Each would have easily survived without the other. Lauper, the rock star, had her fans and wrestling had long had theirs. The sport was selling out large arenas across America before it was on the cover of *Sports Illustrated*. But they did get together and their brief merger seemed to work out.

For many in the public who didn't know one thing about wrestling except they knew they didn't want to know, suddenly, they realized they did want to know. Because everybody was talking about it, they felt like they were missing something.

Wolff went on to produce the Saturday morning cartoon show "Hulk Hogan's Rock 'n' Wrestling." It was this show that helped jettison all of those WWF action figures. Don't call them dolls.

The WWF actually made its official debut on CBS television on September 14, 1985, in all places…Saturday morning cartoons.

"Hulk Hogan's Rock 'n' Wrestling" featured some of the top WWF stars, both animated and even live versions. And Hillbilly Jim was one of them.

It was proof that what had once been a sport often viewed by so called closet fans, had now expanded its tentacles into the kiddie breakfast food circuit. It was marketing at its grandest…get 'em young and they will be with you for a lifetime.

The weekly one hour comedy included three animated cartoons and several live skits by WWF wrestlers. It was uncharted grounds for network television, especially when the 10 a.m. - 11 a.m. time slot is considered Saturday morning prime time.

With Hogan at the center of the episodes, he and his friends and foes stayed true to their "real life" wrestling personalities, with good winning out over evil. The 11 characters were Hulk, Lou Albano, Junkyard Dog, Hillbilly Jim, Andre, Wendi Richter, Tito Santana, Rowdy Roddy Piper, Jimmy Snuka, Nikolai Volkoff, and the Iron Sheik.

(The Cartoon Network on Cable TV in 2016 is further proof that the WWE has entertained itself with promoting to kids. Two hour "Scooby-Doo" shows featuring animated likenesses of McMahon, John Cena, Triple H, and others, continue their fight against evil.)

Hillbilly Jim was right in the middle of it all—not just the wrestling, but also the music.

Remember that guitar his mother had bought for him years before?

What Jim's family lacked in material things, they lacked nothing when it came to their love for music. It looked now like James Henry Morris had suddenly been thrust right smack in the middle of a perfect storm.

"All those years my guitar had been like a dog to me," he said. "Its love was unconditional. It didn't talk back."

In 1986, "The Wrestling (record) Album" was released by Columbia Records Grammy-winning music producer Rick Derringer. He saw little need for a glitzy name on the cover. The visual of the WWF's biggest stars would be enough. And right there with one of the album's three solos was Hillbilly Jim's "Don't Go Messin' With a Country Boy."

"I was proud that I cut the song in one day," Jim said. "Eric Weissberg was the fiddler on it. He did the music for "Deliverance." Les Paul's son, Gene, was the mixing engineer which I think was neat."

The album went quickly up the charts reaching gold status in Canada as did "Piledriver," the follow-up release two years later.

The song would later give Jim a leg up when it came to squeezing his big frame into Nashville's country music business.

"David Wolff was the inspiration behind the album," Jim says. "I was all in as soon as they told me about it. I'm not really sure they knew about my musical ability in the beginning, but I quickly let them know."

It was Derringer and Wolff who wrote and collected some songs they matched with some of the WWF stars.

Then when wrestling manager Jimmy Hart came on board, he brought with him a resume that revealed a lifetime in the music business. In the late '60s he sang with the Gentrys, a group that cranked out teeny bopper songs like "Keep On Dancing." He had toured with the Dick Clark Caravan, The Beach Boys, Sonny & Cher, and appeared on Hullabaloo.

Being from Memphis, Hart hooked up with Jerry Lawler, an old high school classmate, and began managing wrestlers while still producing records. Lawler, recognizing Hart's high energy, included him as a regular ringside character and before long Hart was just as popular as the performers in the ring, becoming widely known as the Mouth of the South.

It was these so-called managers who added to the soap opera drama of a match, often drawing as much exposure both in the arena and on TV, as their "clients."

"Managers were their own business," says Jim. "The agents determined which wrestlers would have managers. For them it was really never about who won or lost. That was pre-determined by the front office…it was all about the performance."

Jimmy Hart's game was abundant energy, constant chatter usually with a hand-held battery-powered megaphone, so that not only could fans near ringside hear what he had to say, but so could those further back in the arena.

Hart could rile a bunch of baby face fans like few others could… except perhaps Bobby "The Brain" Heenan, a wrestler-turned-manager.

"The best shot is a cheap shot. Kick 'em when they're up, kick 'em harder when they're down," Heenan would proudly proclaim.

Most managers were there to create a distraction and became an important part of the show, just as Hillbilly had done when he was rehabbing his injured knee and managing the tag team of Cousin Junior and Uncle Elmer.

The manager's role was usually to distract the referee in order for his guy to unfairly gain the upper hand and win the match. Every move Jimmy Hart made was calculated and planned out as much as possible, just as he had done when choreographing a performance with the Gentrys.

It was Hart's energy that Jim Morris was drawn to. So when he got the call to the WWF, not long after, he told them about Hart.

"The WWF had been trying to get in touch with Jimmy in Memphis. He was managing Lawler," says Jim. "I called him and told him what the WWF was going to do with WrestleMania. They had seen videos of him and liked what they saw. I didn't know if Vince still wanted him or not, so I called them and told them again about Jimmy."

Howard Finkle, the WWF's scheduler and ring announcer, a few minutes later reached Hart.

Hart also had a hand in bringing Randy Savage and Rick Rude to the WWF.

For Hart, Hillbilly Jim's intervention changed his life. And the role Hart played in the music phase of the WWF added a new level to the entertainment. It was Hart who played a key role in developing the ring entrance music for many of the superstars as they made their way to center stage. As soon as the first note came over the huge sound system the entire arena came to its feet. It meant the show was ready to begin.

"I owe my WWF career to Hillbilly," Hart says. "He's the one who got me in."

Hart says he will never forget the first time he saw Jim.

"It was in Memphis," he recalls. "This guy walks in the room and I had to look twice, no, maybe three times. I couldn't believe it. It was a rubberneck moment. Oh sure I'd seen guys as big and bigger, but none with the personality, charisma and showmanship to go along with his size."

Hart also laughs when thinking about how he and Lawler came up with the Harley Davidson name for Jim in his early days in Memphis.

"Jerry and I were in Louisville, sitting in our room at the Red Roof Inn," he said. Jerry was flipping through the pages of the phone book… looking for something that might work for a name. Lawler all of a sudden said, 'here it is, Harley Davidson, we'll make him a biker.'"

Hart's career included managing over 60 wrestler's that included comedian/actor Andy Kaufman.

Years later it was one managing gig that he didn't get that he laughs about.

"Jerry twice ran for the mayor of Memphis and lost," Hart said. "I told him if I'd been his campaign manager he would have won."

Jimmy Hart is still active with the WWE, autograph conventions, action figures, and public appearance. In 2016, he opened Jimmy

Hart's Beach Bar & Grill in Daytona Beach. And what about all of that outlandish clothing he wears?

"Years ago Dick Clark told me, 'If you dress like you are in the audience, then one day you will be in the audience.'"

Requirements to be an effective manager were to be mouthy, crafty, devious and optimistic. While they are crowd favorites, they still draw boos and catcalls. Most managers stoop to the lowest trickery, while a few do it fair and square. Ruthless rule breakers they are called, not caring if they are liked or not. Masters of the underhanded!

Some have been known to flip from managing only heels to baby faces. Call it what you will, but double-crosser and back-stabbers would be a few good words.

Some of the best known managers of Hillbilly Jim's days were Lou Albano, Mr. Fuji, Classy Freddie Blassie, Bobby Heenan, Cyndi Lauper, Johnny Valiant and the Fabulous Moolah. With the exception of Hart and Lauper, the others had actually performed in the ring.

Chapter Fourteen

While it's true that Cyndi Lauper and Andy Kaufman did their share in drawing mainstream attention to wrestling, there were others who liked to be seen with WWF stars, in hopes of catching the wave. Another female entertainer was actually around before Lauper. Deborah Harry, the star of the music group Blondie, was a regular at Madison Square Garden along with Andy Warhol, Joe Piscopo, and Danny DeVito. And on one occasion entertainer Alice Cooper served as Jake "The Snake" Roberts manager for a match. Since both had a fetish for serpents, it probably made sense.

Many came to these matches out of curiosity, but others knowing these wrestlers were drawing sellout crowds everywhere they went, wanted to see, but more importantly, be seen. It was the place to be.

McMahon was a genius, well on his way to crating a billion dollar business. He worked his plan built around story-line soap operas involving super-sized wrestlers with an occasional diva thrown into the fray for good measure. Long gone were the sleazy venues and heavyset guys with soft bodies and very little speed.

"It had started to change when I first came into the business," Jim said. "More and more guys were lifting weights, changing their bodies. Before, it had looked rough and tough, but it was something I wasn't sure I wanted to do."

The WWF was able to blend the so-called giants, the big guys, with the "flyers". The flyers were the guys who had the athleticism of a gymnast and the skills of a high diver.

Even though they weren't 400-pounders, they became very popular and their acrobatics bordered on being almost unbelievable.

One of those flyers was Jumpin' Jimmy Brunzell, a former Minnesota football player, who did many of his moves off the top rope.

"He is such a nice guy and one of my best friends in the business," Jim said. "He was probably too good of a guy to be in the sport."

Brunzell teamed with B. Brian Blair and wrestled tag team as the Killer Bees.

Jimmy "Superfly" Snuka became one of the WWF's biggest stars. With bodybuilder looks and athleticism possessed by few, he was a superstar that appeared in several WrestleManias. It was Snuka who befriended Jim back in Nashville by lending some of his wrestling gear in order for the then Harley Davidson to do a "tryout" match for Pat Patterson and the WWF.

I'd known him from my wrestling beginning," said Jim. "Everybody believed he killed his girlfriend in 1983. Supposedly he kicked her out of his car and she died. They said her daddy was in the Philadelphia mob and was gonna have Snuka killed."

With Snuka one of theWWF's main attraction, Jim says McMahon hired several attorneys to help the star wrestler.

"He went to Tahiti for a couple of years," said Jim about Snuka.

(In September 2015, Snuka, at the age of 72, was arrested for the 1983 murder of Nancy Argentino, as a result of statements he made in his autobiography and then sued the WWE for brain injuries he suffered.)

There were thousands of characters in the business Jim met. Some he stayed as far away as he could, while others became friends. Still, there were others he enjoyed at arms length:

Bobby "The Brain" Heenan was sometime called "The Weasel," depending who he was managing at the time. Bobby also wrestled before becoming one of the superstar managers.

"He is a good friend of mine still today," Jim said of the guy who could affect the outcome of a match by his mere presence with a heel. "He's really having some health issues."

And speaking of the Iron Sheik, Jim says he once was a personal bodyguard for the Shah of Iran before coming to the U.S.

"He wrestled for Iran in the Olympics," Jim said of this character whose entrance into any ring in the country would send the crowd into a rage against him. "It was America against Iran…a natural confrontation anytime the Sheik was in the ring."

Khosrow Vaziri was the Sheik's real name, and Jim says when he came to this country he was very religious.

"He'd been here four or five years when he became one of the biggest sinners," Jim laughed. "It was women, booze, tobacco and drugs. Vince called him in one time and told him he had tested positive on a drug test. Shiek thought that positive meant a good thing."

Jesse "The Body" Ventura was a superstar in the WWF both in the ring and out of it as an announcer. Originally from Minnesota, he would later become governor of that state. At the top of the eccentric list, his colorful wrestling garb included sequins, wraparound shades, tie-dyed clothing, and like Hillbilly Jim, music was his first love. He even released a couple of records and insisted his likeness be embossed into each record "so everyone can see my beautiful body while they hear my beautiful voice."

Ventura, always being a company man in spite of talking like he wasn't, kept the chatter up about his take on Hogan. Once in talking about Hogan, he claimed Hogan was spreading himself to thin to hang onto the belt.

Ventura had this to say:

> "First, he trained that goofball Hillbilly and tried to move him up the ladder too fast. What happened? Johnny Valiant dislocates the Hillbilly's kneecap in San Diego and puts him out of commission. Then he tries to train Mr. T. He isn't concentrating on being the champ, and one of these nights I'm gonna get him."

Gorilla Monsoon was an Ithaca, New York sports hall of famer, and at 400 lbs. he was an early day star when he arrived on the scene in 1963. His outdoor match against Bruno Sammartino in Jersey City, New Jersey was legendary. He was managed at one time by one of the all-time heels, "Wild" Red Berry, and was a tag-team partner with Killer Kowalski. At an over-the-hill age he even subbed for Andre The Giant after Andre broke his ankle in Madison Square Garden. He was highly regarded as a wrestling commentator.

Gene Okerlund, known as "Mean Gene," was anything but mean, and his presence with a microphone in his hand conducting an interview with Vince McMahon about one of the combatants in an up and coming match, in God knows where, gave a bit of sensibility to it all.

Taping promos involving Gene were held weekly for four hours at a time. There were three live shows with 60 wrestlers; two TV shows running simultaneously; two weekly cartoon shows; and a Canadian TV show that ran every two weeks. Gene was directly involved in a total of six hours of weekly promos, not counting the live shows.

Often wearing a tux, he was right in the middle of it all, with facial expressions, and a rolling of his eyes, that revealed a genuine interest in what his 60 second interviews revealed. Mean Gene brought out the best and worst in the gladiators, usually elevating their words to fever pitch. When Gene was finished, fans couldn't wait for the next match.

Okerlund ran an advertising agency in Minneapolis before hooking up with McMahon.

—〰—

Jim had his take on others he knew in and out of the ring.

Andre "The Giant" Rousimoff's name on a wrestling card meant sellout. If anyone could draw like Hogan, it was Andre. At 7-4 and 520 lbs., just the sight of him in the ring put the other wrestlers size in perspective.

"You didn't want to piss him off," Hillbilly Jim said in an understatement. "One night I filled in for Big John Studd against Andre. His body didn't feel human. It felt like hitting cowhide. He wanted me to hit him hard. He called me "boss". He would sign autographs, but not for everyone. I remember he would not sign for Charles Bronson, the actor. Andre never went to a gym, but believe me he could hurt you."

Jake "The Snake" Roberts was another big star always bringing a big cloth sack into the ring with him where he'd place it in one of the corners under the turnbuckle. Everyone in the arena knew what the bag contained, and they also knew what was going to happen when Jake "the Snake" won—which he usually did.

He'd pull his python, named Damien, out and drape it across his fallen opponent to the delight of the crowd.

"He'd rent some of those snakes and some were gentle and some mean," Jim said. "But I saw Andre take the snake after it had bitten him, and pull some of its teeth out of his arm after a match with Jake."

Reebok was all about Andre wearing their shoes. He wore a size 22 and the company said it was the widest they'd ever seen. To further point out how really big he was, *Sports Illustrated* wrote a number of years ago that his fingers were so large that a silver dollar could be passed through one of his rings.

"Andre loved to drink—wine and vodka," says Jim. "And he could get out of hand. He'd be out in clubs and pass out, and his friends couldn't carry him, so they'd leave him on the floor with the piano cover over him."

But there's one Andre story Jim will never forget.

"Andre and I had a Christmas Day match in Miami Beach in 1985," he says. "It was depressing for both of us to be on the road then, especially since we were doing a show the next day in Dayton, Ohio. We got on the plane. I'm over 300 lbs. and crammed into my seat. Andre is well over 500 and you can imagine how he fit in his seat.

"Andre says, 'Boss, lets have a drink'. The flight attendant served us 53 of those little bottles…vodka, bourbon, gin, rum and wine. We drank every bottle they had on the plane. I drank eight and Andre drank the rest. The captain came out to see what the ruckus was about…took one look at Andre and went back in the cockpit.

"Andre carried a metal Halliburton travel case with him when he traveled. He wore the same clothes all of the time, but in his case he had a cribbage game, two decks of cards, and a wine opener."

Jim tells of another Andre encounter, this one in France.

"I think it was around 1986, Andre and I were over there on two different deals in Cannes at the film festival," Jim recalled. "I was doing some exhibition matches in hopes of getting one of their big TV channels to take our product. Andre had two young WWF green-as-grass-first job-just-out-of college guys with him.

"Well, Andre called me at my hotel and invited me to dinner. It was the hotel dining room, a five-star French restaurant. The four of us sat for hours, eating and drinking. We sat so long we were hungry again. Finally when the check came it was $2,000 before tip. I was mad, and the two WWF guys were mortified, because Andre had kept ordering. I could only think what my mama would say if she knew I had eaten a $500 meal (Jim's part). I wanted to slug Andre, but thought better of it. Being from Kentucky, I know little wood from big kindling, and I also know there have been a couple of guys who slugged Andre, and it didn't work out too good for them."

When Andre finally grabbed the check, saying to Jim, "I'll get it, boss," they were all relieved.

"Andre never let anybody pay for anything," Jim said. "Thanks, Andre," I said.

—⟋⟍—

And what about those referees. They often were knocked silly, only to recover just in time to count out or disqualify the wrong guy.

"The referee never gets enough credit for their role," Jim said. "They have to remember where they are at all times in the ring. They have to stay out of the way. But most importantly for them is to remember the finish. The referee is so important and you don't want to leave the outcome up to the them. Don't put the heat on them."

Angelo Poffo, from Lexington, Kentucky, had been in the wrestling business back in the '60s, '70s, and '80s, both as a performer and promoter. Poffo was even said to have the world record for sit-ups at one time, but he became more famous for being the father of Randy and Lanny, who went on to make a mark later in the WWF as Randy "Macho Man" Savage and "Leapin" Lanny Poffo.

For a while it looked like Savage's future would be in baseball, as he spent three years hacking around the minor leagues with the Reds, White Sox and Cardinals. But then he became one of wrestling's biggest stars, teaming with his manager/wife, Miss Elizabeth. Together they were a perfect fit for soap opera storylines in and out of the ring.

Miss Elizabeth was Elizabeth Ann Hulette in real life, from Frankfort, Kentucky. She had done some on-camera TV work after receiving a communication degree from the University of Kentucky.

"Randy was wrestling in Memphis," says Jim. "He was a strange bird...eccentric...didn't trust anybody. He was a sharp businessman and a workaholic, a master in the ring. He wouldn't hurt you for nothing."

Both The Macho Man and Miss Elizabeth's lives were cut short. She died from a drug and alcohol overdose in 2003, and he died in a car wreck in 2011.

Yokozuna wrestled in the early '90s and was said to have weighed 804 lbs. at one time, so naturally the stories about him became legendary.

The WWF ordered him off the road to lose weight when he hit 800 lbs., yet in 1993 it was reported that in one setting he devoured 35 scrambled eggs, a pound of bacon, a large stack of blueberry pancakes and a half-gallon of orange juice. A couple of hours later he was seen eating lunch.

"I really liked him," Jim said. "He was actually from Samoa, and had done some sumo wrestling. One of the great stories on him was when he broke the commode he was sitting on in his hotel. The porcelain under his weight just exploded. Cut his rear bad. The hotel had to call the fire department and use the jaws-of-life to get him out of there."

There were other big guys, too.

Giant Gonzalez was 8-feet in height. "He was from Argentina…a freak of nature," added Jim. "They tried to use him in promos with some midget wrestlers."

The Big Show (Paul Wright) was 7-foot and 450 lbs.; Kevin Nash wrestled as Diesel and had played basketball at the University of Tennessee. He was 6-11 and close to 350 lbs..

Here's a snapshot from Jim as it relates to several others whose path crossed with his:

Ric Flair. He was called "The Nature Boy" and is one of the most recognizable names in wrestling history. I never wrestled against him. I actually met him through my friend, Bruce Swayze. Ric was always smiling and good to me.

Billy Graham was called "Superstar Billy Graham." He was the first really great physique guy in the business. He looked like he had been dropped in from outer space…did lots of pills.

Nikolai Volkoff. The Russian thing made him a natural heel. He was big and clumsy and could accidentally hurt you. Very difficult to have a match with.

George "The Animal" Steele. A dear friend who helped me a lot. He was an old school guy who kept up to date with the profession. One of the smartest guys I ever met. He had been a school teacher and football coach in Michigan. Lots of NFL guys, who had played for him when he was a high school coach, showed up to watch him.

Jesse "The Body" Ventura. He was a rock and roll guy who did security for The Rolling Stones at one time. He was a '60s kind of guy…flamboyant… absolutely out of the box free spirit. He was a big star and treated me great.

Greg "The Hammer" Valentine. He had one speed…slow. When he sped up he was still slow. He was from a wrestling family and never changed his style. I loved wrestling with him because he was one of the real pros in the ring…a true professional. He was a very tough guy.

Johnny Valiant. He's still a character to this day...a survivor for sure. Really knew the business and was always telling me how to cut corners to save money. He saw the business change and didn't spend money on anything he didn't have to. He passed on what he learned to many of us.

Big John Studd. His real name is John Minton. He was a sad story. As big as he was he was paranoid about his size...always wanted to be bigger. He was into the growth hormones and didn't care to give up 10 years of his life to be bigger. He died at the age of 48. Andre didn't like him and would maul him and drag him around when they had a match...really got into John's head. We got along good and had talked not long before he died.

Cowboy Bob Orton. He was from a wrestling family. His dad was a good wrestler. He was superb in the ring. We're still good friends.

Paul "Mr. Wonderful" Orendorff. When I arrived in the business he was a big star...was in the first WrestleMania. He was a Florida guy with a reputation as a street-tough guy. He played some college football. He seemed nervous about everything and had a hair-trigger temper like a bomb ready to go off any time. He got so upset one time he actually pulled the steering wheel off the column of a rental car he had. Told them it just broke. He told me his great body was from good eating. He had the best physique in the business. He got a neck injury and half his body disappeared. We got along great.

Lex Lugar. A 24K asshole...not to me, but the way he treated others. Randy Savage didn't care for him because he thought there was something between Lugar and Miss Elizabeth. Randy was right. He had a great body... a body builder's body... looked good in the ring, but couldn't wrestle. All the boys said he was all show and no go.

Mr. T. I wasn't around him much, but when I was he was nice and polite. He enjoyed the camaraderie of the locker room. Seemed to be in awe of the size of all of the wrestlers. He did lots of promotions with Nancy Reagan about kids staying in school.

Pat Patterson. Great guy...lots of influence in the WWF. Really helped me. He is gay, and proud of it. One of the sharpest minds in the history of wrestling. In his day, Pat was a tag team partner with Ray "The Crippler" Stevens. Pat was the one who brought me that $86,000 check.

—⟁—

And what about perhaps the most infamous wrestling hold in the business...the "sleeper"? Did one wrestler ever really put another one to sleep? How was it that a referee seeing that one of the combatants had locked in on a "sleeper," would determine if the match was over when the victim became lifeless and unable to compete? Most of the time the ref would lift an arm, only to see it fall back down. But on occasion certain wrestlers could come back from "the dead". With finger twitching, arm jerking, someway, somehow, they could overcome the "sleeper" and wake up.

"It was a martial arts thing," says Hillbilly Jim. "Pressure is applied to both sides of the neck, cutting off the flow of blood, putting you to sleep. The wrestlers had to sell it with the hand fluttering and all of that. It was a bullshit hold everybody loved."

Chapter Fifteen

Word spread like wildfire. The magic of TV, especially cable TV, enabled the Vince McMahon WWF machine to unprecedented popularity. And with the advent of WrestleMania the entire family could pay money and watch the event unfold in the comfort of their living room, neighborhood arena or a movie theater. And fans couldn't wait!

WrestleMania was billed as not just the wrestling event of the century, but the sporting event.

The elite of the wrestling world were there and so was an A-list of sports celebrities, entertainers and movie stars. Who would have ever thought it?

Originating live from New York City's Madison Square Garden on March 31, 1985, WrestleMania reached some two million closed-circuit seats in arenas and theaters in North America.

With numbers like this the WrestleMania phenom appeared ready for a long haul. And it was. How could the first one be topped?

WrestleMania II, on April 7, 1986, as only McMahon could do it, originated from three different locations. One was Nassau Coliseum in Long Island, New York. Another was the Rosemont Horizon, in Rosemont, Illinois, and the third, all the way across the country in the Los Angeles Sports Arena. From coast-to-coast it had become a sports spectacular.

The stars were there too. Susan Saint James, Cathy Lee Crosby, spooky queen Elvira, Joan Rivers, baseball's Tommy Lasorda, Darryl Dawkins, jazz legend Cab Calloway, Ray Charles, Ozzy Osbourne, Ricky Schroeder and Robert Conrad.

Hillbilly Jim joined a group of 14 other WWF stars in a Battle Royal against several NFL football plays. Jim Covert, Harvey Martin, Ernie

Holmes, Bill Fralic, Russ Francis and 310-pound William "Refrigerator" Perry were all in the ring at the same time duking it out with the wrestlers.

It had long been questioned; Who's tougher—football players or rasslers? Special referees Dick Butkus of the Chicago Bears and Dallas Cowboy Ed "Too Tall" Jones were brought in as special referees, but even they couldn't prevent Andre "The Giant" from taking it all and being the last man standing. Not even close.

"Those Battle Royals were dangerous," Jim points out. "It was easy to get a knee rolled up, so I usually worked the corners and along the ropes to protect my knee."

These matches were scripted as well, says Jim. Each wrestler had been predetermined when he would be eliminated, usually by being tossed over the top rope and out of the ring.

"Some of them would hurt you and not mean to," he said. "No one wanted to work with someone who was dangerous. Working sometime 60 days in a row, you couldn't afford to get hurt."

Once several of the wrestlers had been eliminated, it opened up more space for three or four to start making more moves and flying around the ring.

WrestleMania III took place March 29, 1987, in Pontiac, Michigan in the Silverdome in front of over 93,000 fans. This was an all-time world indoor attendance record, surpassing a 1981 Rolling Stones concert in the New Orleans Superdome. Closed circuit TV venues such as Madison Square Garden and Toronto's Maple Leaf Garden were also sold out. It was seen worldwide in 26 countries. They wanted to see Hogan against Andre. Millions watched as Hogan won the main event.

Baseball's Bob Uecker, singer Aretha Franklin, TV's Mary Hart and Vanna White were involved in the event in various capacities.

"It was fun," Hillbilly Jim said. "I was teamed with Haiti Kid and Little Beaver, two legendary midget wrestlers. We beat King Kong Bundy and his two midget partners Little Tokyo and Lord Little-brook."

It was the first time in WWF history that there was a six man tag team match with full sized and midgets on each team. Hillbilly's team won on a disqualification, when Bundy squashed Little Beaver.

Other matches included Randy "Macho Man" Savage and his manager and future wife Miss Elizabeth against Ricky "The Dragon" Steamboat, and of course, Rowdy Roddy Piper took on Adorable Adrian

Adonis. Bobby "The Brain" Heenan and Jimmy Hart were also featured attractions as managers.

"I was scheduled to be in the first one if I hadn't of had the knee injury," he said.

Millions and millions of people have seen WrestleMania over the years, and even after Jim wrestled his last official match in 1991, he has returned to be a part of the legends/celebrity group that shows up every year at the request of the WWE.

"I've been to 24 of the 32, representing the WWE in one form or another," he says.

"At the time WrestleMania was cutting edge stuff," says Jim. "It was the biggest show of the year, like our Super Bowl. Every one of us wanted to be on that card. If you were, it meant you were going to be a big part of the WWF's schedule the following year. And that meant more money. WrestleMania was the one event the company pointed to all year."

Jim Morris was a physical marvel. Few in the sport of professional wrestling could match his strength or flexibility, and what he accomplished in his eight years made him one of the most popular wrestlers in the sport's history.

Jim's success as a professional wrestler may have surprised those who knew him as a youngster, and his free spirit personality might have led some to believe his future success would be limited. And for all of those who thought they knew him…they really didn't.

They could see his size—that was rather apparent. But what they couldn't see was his heart and desire to make something out of his life.

"I was driven," he says. "When I locked in on something there was no one who was going to take it away from me. First it was basketball. I played it all the time. I wanted to be the best. Then it was my weight-lifting. I set goals and reached them. I know there were those who thought I'd fail, and that helped drive me. So when the door opened for a career in wrestling, I already had the discipline to put in the time and do whatever it took to be good at it.

"I would have flashbacks of mama raising Dwight and me, and how people felt sorry for us. Heck, it would have been easy for me to feel sorry for myself, but I didn't let that happen. I locked in big time on anything I did to be the best."

Perhaps in no other area of Jim's life was his discipline to not get caught up in his surroundings as a professional wrestler.

"There were drugs, lots of them. And several of the guys were into it, some more than others. In my early days in the business, the WWF didn't test for anything. They just wanted you to be big. Later they began testing for cocaine.

"I was making money, more money than I ever thought possible for me to make, and I aimed to keep it. Some of the guys blew their money on gambling, drugs, cars, booze, jewelry and women. I had a choice to be a little piece of wood or a big load of kindling, and I was smart enough back then to know this show wasn't going to last forever. I had a small window of opportunity and I'm proud to say I've made some good choices."

Early on, no one thought the boy from across the tracks would ever attend college. He did, thanks to people like his high school coach Don Webb; friend Tommy Hagan, who exposed him to weightlifting; Western Kentucky University who permitted him use of their weight room facility even though he wasn't a student; Bill Bunton and Bruce Swayze who made him believe he could be a wrestler. "I had a lot of help along the way," says Jim.

There were others, lots of them. "I've had fame because of all the people who have helped me. And Vince McMahon took an old boy from Kentucky who didn't have anything and turned him into a man who has everything."

Much of Jim's life has revolved around his ability to talk. Going back to those nights when as an 8-year-old, standing on that sawdust floor under a well-worn tent, and with the urging of his mama, he would testify about the Gospel. And he hasn't stopped talking since.

"I've never become greedy with the WWF," said Jim. "I wasn't concerned about what the others were making. I was only concerned about me."

Don't be fooled by all of Jim's chatter. He's a smart guy…always has been. He was smart enough, along the way, to listen to those he knew he could learn from, especially all of those old-school wrestlers.

Jim doesn't argue with the popularity of today's wrestling, though he's not sure he likes it. Those on-and-on story lines, it seems that wrestlers today give little thought of whose watching. The cursing, crotch-grabbing and multiple uses of the middle finger, Jim thinks, take up far more time than wrestling itself.

"The product we see today really doesn't have Vince's thumbprint on it," he says. "In our day there was more real wrestling taking place. It was different then. But back then our TV numbers were unbelievable. A lot of my buddies who wrestled when I did say it was better then. But things change…that's the way life is. Everything has its peaks and valleys, and it looks like the sport is bigger now than it was then. Stephanie McMahon (Vince's daughter), and her husband, wrestler Triple H, run it day to day."

McMahon's daughter turned some of the in-the-ring drama with Triple H into a real husband-wife relationship. He even took on the wrestling name Triple H in a successful effort to twice remove himself from his given name, Paul Michael Levesque. And from there he went to Hunter Hurst Helmsley as his character name. For whatever reason, soon afterward he became Triple H.

"I always tried to lead a clean image because I had a big following of kids, but what some of them are doing in the ring today I think sends a negative message. I still don't think you should take your kids to see all that stuff."

But not wanting to bite the hand that fed him all of those years, Jim is quick to point out that wrestling—professional wrestling, needs to be kept in perspective.

"It's entertainment," he says. "The matches are funny. Are they sending the wrong message? Probably. Do they care? Probably not. Fans get it. They understand it. It's still fun to them."

But then Hillbilly Jim reverted back to Jim Morris and those down home Kentucky roots.

"Don't take it too seriously," he continued. "People try to defend it. Some say I'm a real wrestler. I'm not in the Olympics…never have been. They are real wrestlers. We knew who was going to win when I wrestled and they still do."

Many of the guys, Jim says, are bitter today, wanting the business to be like it was. But it's sort of like not being able to swim in the same ocean twice because the shoreline keeps changing.

"It was horse shit then, and still is now," he says. "It's just more colorful horse shit, but it's still what it is. It's fun…stupid fun. It's great."

Chapter Sixteen

*F*inally, the sport had taken its toll on James Henry Morris. Thousands of body slams, flying mares, double elbow drops, and who knows what else he had been hit with, were layered on top of the 1985 knee surgery, and then the surgery on his neck in 1991 to reduce the pressure from a disc pressing on a nerve that caused him to lose power in his left arm.

Dr. Paul McCombs performed the last operation at Southern Hills in Nashville.

"He was known as the Rock Doctor because he played music while he did his surgeries," said Jim. "That was all right with me. Heck, I like music, too."

In the spring of 1991, Hillbilly Jim performed his last show in Toronto at Maple Leaf Garden. It was a win over Dino Bravo.

Jim had always stuck to professionalism throughout his career, and he never left the ring without giving the fans, no matter how many were there, their money's worth.

"The real professional does the same show in front of 100,000 in Pontiac, Michigan, or 10 in Summer Shade, Kentucky," he said.

His adopted town of Mudlick had been described as a Kentucky holler, two hills back from a moonshine still between Glasgow and Tompkinsville, Kentucky. It was written that it was in Mudlick where he acquired all of those muscles shoveling manure on his family farm. His diet consisted of squirrel and jams, coon and grits, sopping it all up with corn pone biscuits.

It all made good copy and for sure it put money in James Henry's pocket.

The world of professional wrasslin' is all about good and evil, and the millions of fans who showed up across the country and pay their hard earned dollars to crowd into small gyms, warehouses, and anywhere else a ring can be set up, to make sure their favorite good guy gets a fair shake against a snake-handling gladiator, a black-caped warlord or a chain-wrapped barbarian.

Yes, indeed, Hillbilly Jim brought some order to it all, much like Buford Pusser did in the movies. His theatrical naiveté in the ring was perhaps a sign of weakness…until the opening bell rings and the referee declares the match underway.

In the square circle Jim gave no hint of trying to become a world champion. He left the braggadocio stuff, and the loud snarling threats to the crowd seekers. He was there to do his part in taking care of evil.

And evil in the wrasslin' ring came in several different forms. Hair pulling and eye gauging were common and their antics were easily seen by the fans, but for whatever reason not often by the referee. But if you wanted to really see the crowd riled up, let one of the bad guys slip a waded up paper cup from his trunks and poke it into the eyes of the opponent. Or let him at just the right time grab hold of his wrestling tights in order to keep from being pinned.

Jim had always been mindful of his money, driving a 1964 Pontiac Catalina for 12 years. But in 1986 he bought his mother, Opal, a new Lincoln Town car to go along with a new home.

"She deserved it," he says. "I don't know how she did it with Dwight and me. Mama was a heavy smoker and didn't want to smoke in her new car, so she rarely drove it."

Opal Morris died in 1994, ten days after Jim celebrated his 40th birthday. She had seen and enjoyed the success of her oldest son, attending WrestleMania and several of his big shows.

"She was always concerned about my well being in the ring, hoping her boy wouldn't get hurt," said Jim.

James Henry Morris had toured the world, wrestling in Japan, France, Australia, Canada, India, New Zealand and several European countries, and was recognized in all of them. However, it was a California moment he likes to talk about.

"I was walking down Rodeo Drive in Hollywood, and someone driving down the street yelled, 'Hey, Hillbilly Jim,'" he laughed. "Now that was kinda flattering to be recognized like that out on the West Coast, especially on Rodeo Drive."

Hulk Hogan, Jim says, is easily the biggest star to ever perform in professional wrestling. He made the sport what it is today.

"Maybe he stayed too long," he said. "I'm not sure. It's a close call to decide when to quit. So many of the guys were broke, they thought the show would last forever. But it didn't, and a few of them would hang on for one more paycheck. Hogan wasn't one of those, but I'm not sure he left the ring when he should have."

Hogan had appeared in several movies, including Rocky III and on the cover of *Sports Illustrated*, and after McMahon, Jr. bought McMahon, Sr. out in 1982, it was Hogan that was the biggest engine in his wrestling rocket.

It may not be good to ask any wrestler if it's fake. Hogan simply says: "Nine back surgeries, two knee surgeries and two hip surgeries. Does that sound fake?"

Jim Morris feels every morning the price he paid for stardom and big paychecks.

"Some mornings are better than others," he nods. "I just try to keep moving, see a physical therapist regularly and try to work out every day."

And about the fake stuff? "Tom Jones (singer) asked me if wrestling was real? I asked him if his singing was real?"

Even when not in character as Hillbilly Jim, he is bigger than life. In constant demand for autographs, unlike many of the "other sports" superstars, he relishes the notoriety and doesn't shy away from the limelight. He is more than willing to oblige anyone who wants his attention. That's who James Henry Morris has always been.

Jim's meteoric rise in the wrestling profession caught a lot of his friends by surprise and he is quick to say he was in the right places at the right time. And though Jim and some of his old wrestling buddies may not agree with everything going on in the sport, they all agree that financially the WWE is kicking butt.

"Its popularity is at an all-time high," says Jim. "They're blowing it out."

The latest numbers from the WWE verify what he says: 500 million social media followers, including 350 million on its Facebook pages, and 6.4 million subscribers to its YouTube channel. The numbers further show that a city hosting WrestleMania puts more money in the bank than a city hosting the Super Bowl. In 2015, Glendale, Arizona, hosted the mega football event and lost money.

Vince McMahon, wife Linda, and daughter Stephanie have even subjected themselves to several of the storylines, with Vince usually coming across as a heel. And then in 2016, son Shane re-emerged in the business after a couple of years away.

The advent of cable television proved to be the podium from which modern day wrestling could speak. McMahon's aggressive assault to buy out or take out most of the more than 20 territorial promoters throughout the nation brought wrestling under one roof. And that roof is in a fancy headquarters located in Stamford, Connecticut.

In 2013, a Training/Performance Center was opened by the WWE in Orlando. The facility is designed to train future super hero wrestling stars. This developmental program is much more than learning the tricks of the trade in one of the facilities' seven rings.

Long gone are the promoters operating out of a cigar box, with 'rasslers being paid a portion of ticket sales. James Henry Morris caught the big wave of the mid-eighties and became an early part of the new breed with all of those trumped up amenities of a rock star and the salary to go with it.

"I had a decision to make," he says. "I have two knees and I'd already given up one. I only have one neck, so I had a decision to make. Do I have a more complicated surgery that probably would let me wrestle a little longer, risking permanent injury? It wasn't worth it to me."

Jim's popularity as a superstar wrestler allowed him to hit the ground running after his wrestling days were over. Arthur Morowitz owned a company called Coliseum Home Video based out of New York City, and when Jim realized his ring performances might be numbered, he contacted the company about the possibility of working for them.

Jim's status as a WWF star and his personality which was as big as he was, quickly meshed with the video company and he was hired.

"I didn't actually meet Arthur until I was already working for him," said Jim. "Wrestling videos were hot, hot, hot, and Arthur Morowitz was responsible for making Vince McMahon's first million dollars outside of the wrestling shows. When he used to sit down with Vince, Arthur was the wealthy one."

Jim was one of three national sales reps for Coliseum Home Videos and his numbers went through the roof.

One company that dealt with Jim was Wax Works. They were a client located in Owensboro, Kentucky, and later became the official video connection with NASCAR, ESPN, NCAA and NFL to name a few.

Kirk Kirkpatrick was around in the '90s when Hillbilly Jim called him at Wax Works.

"We had Disney World, Warner Bros, Sony, Universal, MGM and the WWF," Kirkpatrick said. "The video stores would be there to buy, and Jim sold them like you wouldn't believe." "Forty to fifty people would stand in line for his autograph and to talk to him."

"There would be vendor shows and Jim would outdraw Playboy Bunnies, Vince Gil, Trisha Yearwood, Kentucky Headhunters, Jim Varney and Rob Lowe."

James Henry Morris never regretted nor apologizes for his Hillbilly Jim character. In fact he is proud of it.

"It's who I am," he says. "What I did in the ring as Hillbilly opened up lots of doors and still does today." "Heck, I went down to Walmart in Arkansas and closed a video deal with them. Then I walked across the street to Sam's Club and closed a deal with them. It was a very lucrative hour and a half for me. In fact, I had two years with Coliseum Videos where I made more money than I ever did in wrestling."

Once Jim was asked, "How can a big ole boy like you sell videos?"

"Well, heck I won't take no for an answer. I'll apply my headlock principle to each sale and clamp on like a duck on a June bug."

In 2005, another door opened for Jim. This time it was a chance to have his own show on Sirius Radio.

"It's called Moonshine Country and airs every Saturday and Sunday," he says.

Before satellite there was Clear Channel and Infinity on the airwaves. Jim remembers it well: "The blues came out of Memphis, rock n roll out of Detroit and Cleveland, and country music in Nashville and Texas."

It was almost a no brainer when Jim's friend, Steve Popovich, Sr., made the wheels turn that led Sirius creative consultant Lil Steven Van Zant to contact Jim. By now Jim was out of the ring, and their connection resulted in the former wrestling star hosting a show on the satellite's Outlaw Country. Van Zant's resume included the Sopranos, and Bruce Springsteen's E Street Band.

"To me Outlaw Country is just about anything you want it to be," he says. "I play Dwight Yoakum, Merle Haggard, Buck Owens, and bluegrass Bill Monroe."

Of course there's a mixture of the new into the old.

"I grew up in this stuff, so it comes easy. I not only know the songs but those who sing them," he adds. "I was an entertainer when I wrestled and I'm an entertainer now. I have a producer, Steve Popovich, Jr., in a Nashville studio, and naturally I get to talk a lot, have some interesting guests, and play some good music."

One of Jim's sounding boards when it comes to music, has been musician Ken Smith. Smith who goes by the stage name of Kenny Lee has toured with several national groups, and because he, too, lives in Bowling Green, Hillbilly Jim and Kenny Lee have become well known on the local music scene.

"My first memory of Jim was as a bouncer," Smith continues. "I played music in some of those places. He was what I called one of those musclemen. I remember, too, at a gym where I went they had a picture of him on the wall."

Smith and Jim's friendship grew and they soon realized they had a love for not just any music, but blues in particular.

"I had a group that toured the country and when we were back in Bowling Green and played, I'd ask Jim to sit in with us," recalls Smith. "And, believe it or not when we were on the road he'd show up and perform with us."

With Jim's promotional savvy he always seemed to take advantage of his Hillbilly Jim popularity all over the country.

"Jim was easily recognized every time he played with us," says Smith. "He carried pictures of his wrestling days and people would line up to meet him and get his autograph. It was unbelievable."

Smith, who is talented on the piano, keyboard and guitar, has a resume that includes performing with super-picker Sam Bush and New Grass Revival, and Duck Butter that included Bush, John Cowan, Jeff Jones and Byron House. He took full advantage of the Les Paul guitar he got back in 1970, and has over the years become a nationally known musician. So when he says James Henry Morris is more than a muscleman, he knows what he is talking about.

"He played with a group who called themselves Hoo Doo Men... Jim and Steve Ford. They were pretty good," Smith says.

"Jim could easily front his own band. His people skills and business sense have permitted him to be successful. He gets so focused in everything he has ever done. He's like a big neon sign when he walks into a room or ring or stage. He's a great musician," Smith said. "A lot of local people don't know that Jim has recorded songs on an album that went gold."

Jim's musical accomplishments have been overshadowed by his wrestling history. He has recorded with Cyndi Lauper, played in the New Orleans Jazz Festival, Chicago Blues Festival ("I played the House of Blues in L.A. before Clapton did.")

Because Jim always seems to be in a live action mode, over the years he has done such a good job of being Hillbilly Jim, that he is asked lots of questions about...well, about being a hillbilly.

"What's the most hillbilly thing you've done lately?" he was asked.

"I went to a buddy's farm and watched him work," replied Jim. "He was doing some mowing, I sat on his porch with a Bud and watched him mow the yard. I could have watched him do that forever."

Another question was, "What's the official policy on moonshine since you are from Kentucky?"

"It's mandatory," answered Jim. "Being from Kentucky I tasted it one time. Some buddies of mine tried to make their own. It tasted like rubbing alcohol. 'I said, I ain't drinking that shit—I'll be blind by morning.'"

In the middle of 2010 Jim got a call from the WWE asking him if he would like to be a part of a hangout reunion with some of his old wrestling buddies. It had been almost 20 years since his last official match, except for an occasional WrestleMania appearance, but he had stayed connected through being a sales rep in the home video business. Then he came back to the WWE as the tag team "manager of record" for the Godwins, Phenius and Henry. They were supposedly a couple of good ole boys from down Arkansas way, and with Hillbilly Jim keeping a sharp lookout for them, they won the WWE tag team title in 1993. After that, he returned to wrestling video sales. "My staying a part of the WWF actually helped with video sales," he said.

Jim listened to what plans the WWE had in store for their reunion show and he liked it.

"It was a reality show they were going to do called Legends House," he says. "There would be eight of us and we'd all be put together for about 21 days to video a 12 episode show that would air on the WWE channel where it would be one of the anchor shows."

The legends joining Jim were Jimmy Hart, Hacksaw Jim Duggan, Tony Atlas, Pat Patterson, Roddy Piper, Gene Okerlund and Howard Finkle.

Located in Rancho Mirage, California, a suburb of Palm Springs, it was reported some $2 million was spent on production, and that included staging the home with a pool, tennis court and appropriate furnishings.

"No expenses were spared," Jim said. "The house was on the historic register and once belonged to Harpo Marx. We didn't want for anything. All kinds of food and liquor were flowing."

Even though the home was beautiful, and the group, as part of the show, was paid a visit from actors Gary Busey and Adam West, Jim said it was 'sort of like being in jail.'

"We were mic'd day and night and didn't have access to a phone, computer, TV or newspaper," he added. "That was a real downer considering we were there for those 21 days beginning in late February. That meant we couldn't watch the NCAA basketball tournament.

"When you're with someone that long, you really get to know them," Jim said. "I thought I knew them, but I really didn't."

The producers of the show had something planned everyday for the group…usually away from the house in order to get a video shoot in. One of those shoots created a memorable episode in Legends House that Jim Morris still talks about.

"We went to Vegas," he said. "We were all going to become Chippendale Dancers. It was unreal and they were filming it all. We went to a spa…shaved, waxed, manicures, spray tans, you name it and we all had it done to us. We rehearsed with the Chippendale guys and when we actually did the show the ladies went wild. They were handling us like cops handling a donut."

"It was in the can for two years," says Jim. "They (WWE) were trying to decide what to do with it. Vince wanted $200,000 an episode, and the cable channels said that was too much."

Jim was paid $50,000 for the project, and the show finally aired in 2013.

Hillbilly Jim is still a marketing force when it comes to wrestling legends. From his WrestleMania appearances, being a commentator, trade shows, conventions, promotions and Fan Axxess Tours, he is still in demand.

Though the powerful adrenaline rushes he first experienced at those tent revivals, and the ones in front of thousands of people at WrestleMania might no longer be there, he still relishes those days that have made him who he is today.

His high school senior yearbook gave not a single indication of his future success. Only his name, James Morris, appeared near a photo.

There was one problem, however. Although it was a posed picture of a young man in coat and tie, it was not James Henry Morris. But the photo of the James Morris in the yearbook had glasses, too.

"It was not me," Jim said. "There was another James Morris in my class. In school he went by James and I went by Jim…and besides that I didn't own a coat or tie and never posed for a yearbook picture."

Jim was also missing from all of the senior class accolades that included "best physique," "most talented," "most athletic," "most congenial," "best personality," most talkative," "most unique," and "most likely to succeed."

It was ironic that when he showed up for his ten-year class reunion, he could have easily qualified for all of these.

"At the reunion, I was voted "Most Changed for the Better," Jim says.

For the first ten years following high school, for most, the search is on for the future. And after a sluggish start, Jim focused in on his building a solid foundation for what was to come.

Decades have passed since he was unable to walk the graduation line at his high school because of grades. So it seemed only fitting that in 2000, that same school named him to its Hall of Honor.

Conclusion

Jim was a contradictory within himself…always has been. He relished his new Hillbilly Jim identity, reaching the top tier of his chosen sport. He immersed himself into his assigned "character," both in and out of the ring.

Deep down, however, Jim Morris knew he wasn't the Jethro Bodine character he projected in the ring. Though the hillbilly aspect was not that much of a stretch because of his rural Kentucky upbringing, he could easily dial in on a family member or two and a few local personalities that added depth to the image he was projecting.

Away from it all, when the bright lights were turned off and Jim's aw-shucks, toothy smile was no longer on the TV screen, a sophisticated, more cosmopolitan personality peaked through it all. A gift-of-gab that had served him well all of his life became his calling card, especially out of the ring.

As an entertainer he had created someone he was really not, and through it all he had remained true to himself. Never forgetting who he was and where he came from, he kept the same friends, despite his fame and success as a world-known sports star.

Somewhere in it all that eight-year-old boy, James Henry Morris, is still locked inside. He would trudge into the dark night to a neighbor's house in search of a phone to summon a doctor for his sick mother, knowing that his effort could depend on her survival.

Reverting back to those days as a young boy he says: "I never felt safe. I was scared. I was a little boy with no father and no big brother, and it was scary walking out into a dark night. I always felt like the wheels could run off in my life at anytime."

Perhaps the single biggest reason Jim was able to survive in his uncertain world is his ability to channel his passions into something productive.

Anyone who ever met him, away from the Hillbilly Jim character, quickly recognizes his intellect. In fact, the depth of his intelligence and knowledge, far out distance the high school diploma he received back in 1971, several weeks after his classmates had already walked the line. His street-wise savvy is only matched by the book smarts he has accumulated while traveling the world.

Those passionate testimonials at the tent revivals, playing basketball until he could play no more, becoming a champion weightlifter, jumping head first into, of all things, professional wrestling and becoming one of the sport's biggest stars, and then turning it all into something special…the Hillbilly Jim story.

Epilogue

*H*onored and embarrassed. These were the two feelings I had when Gary West told me he wanted to do a book on my life. I thought it was a rib or a joke! I soon found out how serious Gary was about this, so, here we are.

I have some things that I wish to say that are not in this book to my children and grandchildren.

To my kids, I love you all so much and I'm so proud of the men and women you've become. I've always tried, and still do, as best I can to keep you apart from my celebrity. It's because of my lack of trust and suspicion of people I don't know. I'm not comfortable with people knowing so much about my life, my family and friends. To me, if everyone knows your business then you have no business.

My grandchildren, at the present time, number eight and one half, and holding. I hope you all are wonderful people and have a great life.

To my brother, niece, and to all of my mother's family, thanks for being great to me, and for the most part always supporting whatever project I came up with.

I had wonderful aunts, uncles and cousins on my mother's side. The best! I didn't get to know any on my father's side. They were never around. So, to any of these relatives I'm sorry we never got to know each other. I just don't feel the need to try and catch up after a lifetime of not knowing them. After all, I was just a kid with no way of reaching out to them, and that ship has already sailed.

Thank God for a great mother and her family.

Many of my friends are mentioned in this book, but there are others.

We didn't say enough about my buddy, Bob Sanborn, one of my oldest and best friends. Thanks Bob. Arthur and Harriet Morowitz, I love you both and your family. My dear friend Marty Applebaum; "Jumpin" Jim Brunzell and his wife Mary, from the great state of Minnesota. Jim thanks for the kind chapter in your book "MatLands." Also, thanks to my guru Steve Ford and his brother Tim. Thanks to my producer of my Sirius XM Radio show "Moonshine Matinee" Steve Popovich, Jr., to Brittany his wife, and their sons. We're into our eleventh year doing this show. It would not have been possible without Steve's legendary father, Steve Popovich, Sr., who had the vision to put this show together for me. I miss this man and think of him weekly.

By the way, as I started thinking of people I wanted to mention, I realized it would probably be almost everyone I ever spent any time with. I can't possibly mention you all. Just know as long as I'm alive I'll never forget what you mean to me. Thanks to Sturgil, Stoner, Pat Haney, Jack Sheidler, Bruce Spence, and man, I still miss my buddy Brent.

I want to make this very clear. I wish I could have another lifetime to just exercise and workout the right way. It takes a lifetime to just figure it out. And then your time is up. What a shame!

I get up every day and try. That's the secret. Nothing is more important than your health... not fame, not fortune, not possessions. If you have your health then everything is possible. Someday, sooner or later, my time will be up and people will say well, I thought he exercised and worked out all the time, but he still died! Those folks don't get it. I'm not interested in the quantity of life, I'm interested in the quality of life. Heredity is so important in living a long time. Exercise and nutrition improves the quality of ones life.

To the wrestling business, let me just say this. The pro wrestling business is one of the best on earth with some of the worst people in it on earth! I did not get caught up in all the trappings of that business. I was there for a reason, not a season. I did it for money, and, I treated it as a job, not a lifestyle.

I've instructed my children that if I die before I'm inducted into the WWE Hall of Fame, do not accept it. I despise those posthumous inductions. Give a person their flowers while they are alive so they can enjoy them.

I talked to one of my best friends Bruce Hart from the famous Hart wrestling family in Calgary, Canada. He's a true genius about pro wrestling. I told him I only live in the now, there is no such thing as the future.

Take care of now and you will all have a better life.

Thanks for doing this Gary West. Love to you and Deborah.

Jim Morris, aka Hillbilly Jim

About the Author

Gary P. West has simple criteria when it comes to writing books.

"I only take on a project that I will enjoy writing about and I only write about something I think people will enjoy reading," he says.

West grew up in Elizabethtown, Kentucky and attended Western Kentucky University before graduating from the University of Kentucky in 1967 with a journalism degree. At U.K. he was a daily sports editor for the Kentucky Kernel.

Later he served as editor for the nation's largest civilian enterprise military newspaper at Fort Bragg, North Carolina. From there he was employed in the corporate advertising office of one of the country's largest insurance companies, State Farm Insurance in Bloomington, Illinois, where he was a copywriter.

He returned to Kentucky in 1972 where he began an advertising and publishing business.

Along the way, for twelve years, he was the executive director of the Hilltopper Athletic Foundation at Western Kentucky University, and provided color commentary for Wes Strader on the Hilltopper Basketball Network.

In 1993, he became the executive director of the Bowling Green Area Convention and Visitors Bureau. He retired from there in 2006 to devote more time to his writing.

He is a freelance writer for several magazines in addition to writing a syndicated newspaper travel column, *Out & About...Kentucky Style*, for several papers across the state.

Gary is in demand as a speaker and for book signings throughout Kentucky.

This is his tenth book. Previous books are *King Kelley Coleman: Kentucky's Greatest Basketball Legend* (2005), *Eating Your Way Across Kentucky* (2006), *Eating Your Way Across Kentucky – The Recipes* (2007), *Shopping Your Way Across Kentucky* (2009), *101 Must Places to Visit in Kentucky Before You Die* (2009), co-authored *Kentucky Colonels of the American Basketball Association: The Real Story of a Team Left Behind* (2011), *The Boys From Corbin: America's Greatest Little Sports Town* (2013), and *Better Than Gold: Olympian Kenny Davis and the Most Controversial Basketball Game in History* (2014) and *Road Trip Eats* (2015).

Gary and his wife, Deborah, live in Bowling Green, Kentucky.

Index

A

Adonis, Adorable Adrian 113, 212
Afflis, William Fritz 12
Albano, Captain Lou 131, 133,
    194, 195, 197, 200
Ali, Muhammad 90, 119, 129
American Wrestling Association 94
Anderson, John 138
Andre The Giant 77, 97, 99, 105,
    120, 197, 203, 212
Angle, Kurt 110
Applebaum, Marty 188, 230
Argentino, Nancy 202
Arum, Bob 90
Atkins, Tony 44
Atlas, Tony 223
Austin, Stone Cold Steve 170

B

Backlund, Bob 126
Bailey, Albert 189
Bastine, Red 186
Bazzell, Jimmy 31
Beckner, David 59
Beefcake, Brutus "The Barber" 17,
    18, 19, 23
Bellomo, Salvatore 99
Bell, Ricky 59
Berle, Milton 120
Berry, "Wild" Red 12, 203
Big Show, The 207
Big Vadar 175
Birdsong, Otis 81
Blair, B. Brian 144, 202
Bland, Donnie 42, 44, 59
Blanton, Otis 29
Blassie, Classy Freddie 12, 120,
    187, 200
Blue Star Ranger Band 29
Bockwinkle, Nick 142

Bollea, Terry 18, 121
Borrone, Bert 39, 42
Boston, George 27
Bowden, Rhea 59
Bowling Green Business College
    83
Bowling Green High School 31,
    36, 38, 39, 40, 55, 65, 81
Boys Club 36, 37
Bravo, Dino 217
Brett, George 123
British Bulldogs 148
Britt, Johnny 41, 59
Bronson, Charles 204
Brown, Goldman 25
Brunzell, Jumpin Jimmy 149, 201,
    230
Brunzell, Mary 230
Buntin, Bill 82, 89
Bunton, Bill 214
Bunton, Granville 84
Busey, Gary 224
Bush, Sam 222
Butkus, Dick 136, 212

C

Cain, Chris 168
Calhoun, Haystacks 194
Calloway, Cab 211
Cameron College 64, 81
Campbell, Glen 172
Campbell, Lloyd 33, 38, 43, 54,
    59, 162
Cardwell, Frank 42, 43, 44
Carter, Jimmy 85
Carter, Maybelle 29
Carter, Ron 64
Carter, Steve 32, 33, 37, 39, 40,
    41, 45, 59, 62, 81, 162
Cena, John 197

Chapman, Marshall 181
Charles, Ray 124, 211
Checker, Chubby 124
Chumbul, Luby 189
Clark, Dick 9, 195, 200
Clemmons, Clarence 167
Coleman, Wayne 180
Coliseum Home Video 156, 220
Collins, Charles 36, 37
Conlee, John 124
Conrad, Robert 211
Cook County Convention Center 99
Cooke, Phil 33, 59
Cooper, Alice 201
Costas, Bob 142
Cousin Alford 91
Cousin Junior 22, 23, 91, 126, 198
Cousin Luke 23, 154
Covert, Jim 211
Cowan, John 222
Cowboy Jack 164, 181, 189
Cow Palace 22
Crosby, Cathy Lee 211
Crum, Denny 83

D

Daniels, Charlie 177
Davidson, Steve 64
Davis, Kenny 192
Dawkins, Darryl 211
Day, Russ 48, 61
Dean, Dizzy 10
Delafield School 28
Denton, Dave 83
Derringer, Rick 197
DeVito, Danny 110, 201
DiBiase, Ted 172
Dick "The Bruiser" 11, 12, 120
Diddle Arena 41, 42, 43, 44, 119
Diesel 207
Dillon, J.J. 98
Dirty Rhodes 69, 95, 112
Dorn, Joel 130
Doughty, Larry 31, 32, 39, 40, 81
Dr. Death 112, 113
Duck Butter 222
Duggan, Hacksaw Jim 146, 223
Duncan, Tommy 33, 40, 43, 54, 59

E

Earth Quake 185
E.B. Terry Elementary School 26, 52

Eddy, Duane 179
Ellis, James 64
Elvira 211
Elvis 141
England, Stan 36

F

Fabulous Moolah 124, 169, 194, 200
Farm Aid 138, 139
Farris, Wayne 97
Ferrigno, Lou 121
Finkle, Howard 9, 199, 223
Fishback, Charles 41, 59
Fishback, Daymeon 42
Flair, Ric 114, 181, 207
Fogerty, John 174
Ford, Steve 150, 167, 222, 230
Ford, Tim 150, 189, 230
Foster, Bill 48, 60
Fralic, Bill 134, 212
Francis, Russ 212
Franklin, Aretha 212
Franks, Ken 113
Frazier, Stan 22
Freedom Hall 40
Fuji, Mr. 200
Funk, Terry 180

G

Gagne, Vern 11, 12
Gaines, Jerry "Peanut" 118, 119, 178
Garibaldi, Gino 12
Gatti, John 100
Gentrys 198
Georgetown College 83
Giant Gonzalez 207
Gibbs, Terry 109
Gil, Vince 221
Girondo, Vince 133
Godwin, Henry 223
Godwin, Phenius 223
Godwins, The 76, 156
Golden, Sterling 97
Gorgeous George 12, 111, 119, 121, 122
Gorilla Monsoon 76, 105, 203
Goulet, Sgt. Rene 109, 110
Graham, Eddie 98
Graham, Otto 10
Graham, Superstar Billy 180, 207
Gray, Paul 190
Griffin, James 42, 44, 59

Grow, Brad 59
Gulas, Nick 89, 91

H

Haddox, James 64
Hagan, Mike 151
Hagan, Tommy 34, 35, 82, 84, 151, 214
Haggard, Merle 221
Haiti Kid 76, 212
Hall, Jerry 64
Haney, Pat 230
Harley Davidson 6, 8, 68, 94, 95, 98, 100, 199
Harpool, Ernie 38
Harris, Linda 73
Harris, Tom 18, 19, 73, 80
Harry, Deborah 201
Hart, Bret 93, 184
Hart, Bruce 230
Hart, Jimmy "Mouth of the South" 6, 9, 22, 142, 165, 171, 176, 188, 198, 199, 213, 223
Hart, Martha 139
Hart, Mary 212
Hart, Owen 93, 94, 139, 188
Harts, The 99
Hart, Stu 93, 142
Haskins, Clem 84
Haynes, Billy Jack 149
Heater, Terry 59
Heenan, Bobby "The Brain" ("The Weasel") 75, 76, 105, 106, 109, 114, 169, 185, 198, 200, 202, 213
Heggie, Tommy 99
Heiner, Phil 59
Helmsley, Hunter Hurst 215
Henderson, Tom 81
Hershey Park Arena 149
Heston, Charlton 158
Hill, Gayle 83
Hindman, Vicky 132
Hogan, Hulk 7, 9, 12, 17, 18, 22, 23, 75, 78, 86, 97, 103, 104, 106, 107, 109, 111, 117, 120, 121, 126, 128, 133, 137, 142, 155, 165, 197, 203, 212, 218
Holmes, Ernie 211
Honky Tonk Man 97, 180
Hoo Doo Men 222
Houchens, Henry 89
Houchens, Opal 25
Houchens, Trudy 73, 89

House, Byron 222
House of Blues 159
Howe, Gordie 167
Hulette, Elizabeth Ann 206

I

Inoki, Antonio 90
Iron Sheik 97, 121, 135, 182, 185, 197, 202

J

James, Susan Saint 211
Jaycee Pavilion 67, 92
Jenner, Bruce 141
Jennings, Waylon 124
Johnson, Albert 26, 27
Johnson, Stan 64
Jones, Alamo 181, 189
Jones, Dwight 81
Jones, Ed "Too Tall" 212
Jones, George 124, 163
Jones, Jeff 222
Jones, Tom 219
Junkyard Dog 99, 113, 137, 197

K

Kaufman, Andy 94, 95, 199, 201
Keady, Gene 86
Kean, Luscious Lanny 22, 91, 92
Kentucky Headhunters 166, 221
Killer Bees 202
Killer Kowalski 203
King Kong Bundy 23, 80, 212
Kirkpatrick, Kirk 220
Knight, Larry 64
Koch, Ed 132

L

Langley, Don 103
Larson, Mike 32, 48
Lasorda, Tommy 211
Lauper, Cyndi 133, 193, 194, 195, 196, 200, 201, 223
Lawler, Jerry "The King" 8, 10, 68, 94, 95, 98, 100, 111, 126, 168, 198, 199
Lawrence, Keith 126
Lawson, Richard 59
Lee, Buddy 124
Leech, Robin 157
Lee College 83
Lee, Kenny 187, 222
Legends House 223, 224
Leone, Baron Michele 12

Letterman, Dave 94, 95
Levesque, Paul Michael 215
Lewis, Gene 23, 154
Lewis, Guy 81
Lewis, Jerry Lee 124
Liberace 119, 131
Ligon, Tyree 64
Lindsey, George (Goober) 125,
    140
Little Beaver 76, 212
Little Richard 154
Little Tokyo 212
Lord Alfred Hayes 105, 169
Lord Little-brook 212
Los Angeles Sports Arena 211
Louisville Invitational Tournament
    40
Lowe, Rob 221
Lugar, Lex 208

M

Madison, Billy 47
Madison Square Garden 113, 119,
    146, 148, 195, 211, 212
Mann, Dale 72, 91, 93, 110
Mansfield, Eddie 113
Manson, Cal 93
Maple Leaf Garden 212, 217
Markham, Stan 33, 37, 38, 43, 44,
    56, 62, 81
Martin, Billy 119, 131
Martin, Harvey 134, 211
Marx, Harpo 224
McCombs, Paul 217
McCormick, Craig 86
McDaniels, Jim 28, 36, 41, 42
McKinney, Greg 59
McMahon, Linda 71, 219
McMahon, Shane 220
McMahon, Stephanie 215, 219
McMahon, Vince 6, 13, 21, 74, 99,
    101, 103, 106, 108, 109, 110,
    111, 117, 119, 120, 121, 122,
    144, 153, 195, 197, 201, 202,
    203, 211, 214, 219, 220
McMahon, Vince, Jr. 193
McMahon, Vince, Sr. 90, 97
McNeill, W.R. 32
Meadors, Bill "Yogi" 85
Meat Loaf 125
Memphis Coliseum 95, 96
Merrell, Ray 64
Miken, George 10
Miller, Red 81

Million Dollar Man 172
Minton, John 208
Miss Elizabeth 206, 208, 212
Moffat, Butch 93
Monroe, Bill 124, 221
Moonshine Country 221
Moonshine Matinee 230
Morowitz, Arthur 164, 188, 220,
    229
Morowitz, Harriet 229
Morris, Dwight 25, 26, 27, 28, 29,
    33, 35, 51, 52, 53, 108, 191
Morris, Gayle 96
Morris, Opal 26, 27, 28, 48, 49,
    50, 62, 81, 144, 218
Morris, William E. 25
Motorhead 173
Mr. Fuji 146
Mr. T 120, 128, 137, 203, 208
Mullendore, David 33, 59
Mulligan, Black Jack 98

N

Nash, Kevin 207
Nashville Municipal Auditorium
    99
Nassau Coliseum 148, 211
National Wrestling Alliance 98
Nature Boy, The 207
Nelson, Willie 124
New Grass Revival 222
New Haven Coliseum 99
Nowinski, Chris 176

O

Odemns, Mike 84
Oglesby, Burch 85, 86
Okerlund, Mean Gene 171, 203,
    204, 223
Oldham, Bill 59
Oldham, John 48
Ongst, Gary 176
Orendorff, Paul "Mr. Wonderful"
    114, 120, 127, 131, 208
Orton, Cowboy Bob 208
Osbourne, Ozzy 211
Outback Jack 137
Outlaw Country 221
Owens, Buck 221

P

Patera, Ken 105, 106, 137, 146
Patterson, Pat 99, 112, 113, 120,
    202, 208, 223

Paul, Gene 197
Paycheck, Johnny 139
Perry, William "Refrigerator" 212
Philbin, Regis 143
Pickens, Jim 33
Piper, Rowdy Roddy 11, 120, 127, 128, 176, 186, 195, 197, 212, 223
Piscopo, Joe 110, 201
Poffo, Angelo 206
Poffo, Leapin Lanny 181, 206
Popovich, Brittany 230
Popovich, Steve, Jr. 125, 163, 189, 222, 230
Popovich, Steve, Sr. 124, 125, 221, 230
Pride, Charlie 163
Prine, John 164

R

Race, Harley 114
Ragland, Dwight 62, 81
Ragland, Frank 32, 33, 36, 38, 39, 40, 41, 45, 59, 62, 64, 81, 82, 161
Reagan, Nancy 208
Redman, Kevin 33
Redmon, Chet 32
Redmon, Kevin 59
Reese, Pee Wee 10
Reeves, Del 141
Reid, Jim 83
Reubin, Martin 33
Rhodes, Dusty 173, 186
Richards, Jim 48
Richter, Wendi 194, 197
Ricky "The Dragon" Steamboat 212
Rivers, Joan 211
Rivers, Johnny 124, 172
Roberts, Jake "The Snake" 177, 201, 204
Robinson, Jim 38
Rocca, Antonio 11, 120
Rock 'n' Wrestling 193
Rock, The 9, 184
Rodes, John B. 25
Rogers, Nature Boy Buddy 94, 120
Rolling Stones, The 207
Rosemont Horizon 211
Rotunda, Mike 142, 148
Rousimoff, Andre "The Giant" 204

Ruben, Martin 59
Rude, Rick 199

S

Sammartino, Bruno 182, 194, 203
Sanborn, Bob 21, 189, 229
Sanderford, Paul 119
San Diego Sports Arena 17, 18
Santana, Tito 197
Savage, Randy "Macho Man" 181, 199, 206, 208, 212
Scarpa, Joe 22, 100, 183
Schroeder, Ricky 211
Schultz, David 112, 113
Scott, George 100
Scuffling Hillbillies 91, 100
Sharpe Cabrillo Hospital 18
Sharp, Iron Mike 113, 150
Shearon, Doug 64
Sheidler, Jack 230
Silverdome 212
Sinks, Bill 64
Skaggs, Boz 125
Skoland, Arnold 146
Smith, Ken 222
Smith, Roger 95, 96
Snuka, Jimmy "Superfly" 99, 197, 202
Snyder, John 59
Special Delivery Jones 105, 106
Spence, Bruce 230
Spivey, Danny 113, 134
Stampede Wrestling 93
Steele, George "The Animal" 175, 207
Stevens, Ray "The Crippler" 174, 208
St. Joe Gym 83
St. John, Michael 91
Stone Cold 9
Stoner 230
Stossel, John 113
Strader, Wes 118, 119, 178
Strongbow, Chief Jay 22, 23, 100, 104, 108, 112, 114, 183
Stuart, Brill 85
Stuart, Howard 85
Stuart, Jesse 85
Stuart, John 85
Studd, Big John 99, 105, 106, 120, 145, 204, 208
Sturgil 230
Sublett, John 64
Swayze, Bonnie 98, 162

Swayze, Beautiful Bruce 89, 91,
    92, 98, 99, 124, 162, 167, 178,
    207, 214
Swit, Loretta 124, 143

T

Taylor, Freddie 64
Taylor, Terry 182
Tenta, John 185
Thesz, Lou 12
Thomas, Rico 187
Thompson, Linda 141
Titan Sports (WWF) 70
Toombs, Roderick George 127
Triple H 197, 215
Tug Boat 169

U

Uecker, Bob 135, 212
Ultimate Warrior 145
Uncle Elmer 22, 23, 74, 126, 198

V

Valentine, Greg "The Hammer" 23,
    99, 207
Valiant, "Handsome" Jimmy 171
Valiant, Lucious Johnny 17, 18,
    19, 171, 200, 203, 208
Vanderbilt's Memorial Gymnasium
    40
Van Zant, Steven 189, 221
Varney, Jim 221
Vaziri, Khosrow 202
Ventura, Jesse "The Body" 126,
    131, 203, 207
Voight, John 158
Volkoff, Nikolai 121, 182, 197, 207
Vol State 83

W

Wagner, George Raymond 121
Ware, Koko B. 165
Warhol, Andy 110, 201
Weasel, The 202
Webb, Don 32, 33, 34, 38, 39, 40,
    42, 44, 45, 47, 56, 59, 62, 81,
    160, 161, 214
Webber, Randy 93

Weissberg, Eric 197
Welch, Roy 91
West, Adam 224
West, Deborah 192, 230, 232
Western Kentucky University 84,
    214
West, Gary 192, 229, 231, 232
White, Vanna 212
Williamson, Fred "The Hammer"
    183
Wilson, Jim 113
Windham, Barry 142, 148
Wolff, David 194, 195, 196, 197
World Wrestling Entertainment
    (WWE) 13, 188, 197, 199,
    202, 213, 219, 220, 223, 224,
    230
World Wrestling Federation (WWF)
    8, 9, 12, 13, 17, 18, 20, 21, 22,
    23, 97, 98, 99, 100, 101, 103,
    104, 105, 106, 107, 110, 112,
    113, 114, 115, 117, 118, 119,
    120, 121, 123, 124, 126, 127,
    134, 137, 151, 154, 165, 176,
    181, 193, 194, 195, 196, 197,
    198, 199, 201, 202, 203, 205,
    206, 208, 211, 212, 214, 220,
    221, 223
WrestleMania 173, 175, 196, 199,
    208, 213, 219, 223, 224
WrestleMania 17 184, 185
WrestleMania I 119, 120, 131, 211
WrestleMania II 134, 135, 144,
    211
WrestleMania III 76, 212
Wright, Paul 207

Y

Yamamoto, Tojo 89, 92
Yearwood, Trisha 221
Yoakum, Dwight 221
Yokozuna 206
Young, Mae 169

Z

Zbyszko, Larry 182
Zhukof, Boris 79
ZZ Top 160

Other books by Gary P. West

WWW.ACCLAIMPRESS.COM

**Eating Your Way Across Kentucky: 101 Must
  Places to Eat**
232 pages • 6x9 (hardcover) • $21.95
ISBN: 978-0-9790025-1-9

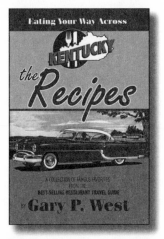

Eating Your Way Across Kentucky: the Recipes
224 pages • 6x9 (hardcover) • $24.95
ISBN: 978-0-9798802-3-0

**Shopping Your Way Across Kentucky: 101
  Must Places to Shop**
232 pages • 6x9 (hardcover) • $21.95
ISBN: 978-1-935001-11-9

**101 Must Places to Visit in Kentucky Before
  You Die**
232 pages • 6x9 (hardcover) • $24.95
ISBN: 978-1-935001-29-4

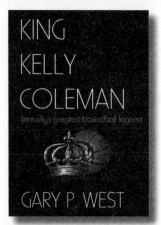

King Kelly Coleman: Kentucky's Greatest Basketball Legend
192 pages • 6x9 (hardcover) • $21.95
ISBN: 978-0-9773198-0-0

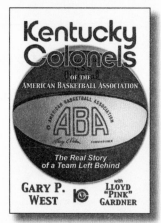

Kentucky Colonels of the American Basketball Association: The Real Story of a Team Left Behind
352 pages • 7x10 (hardcover) • $24.95
ISBN: 978-1-935001-82-9

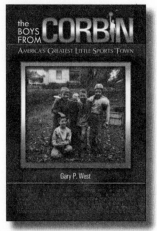

The Boys From Corbin: America's Greatest Little Sports Town
320 pages • 6x9 (hardcover) • $24.95
ISBN: 978-1-938905-23-0

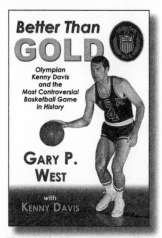

Better Than Gold: Olympian Kenny Davis and the Most Controversial Basketball Game in History
304 pages • 6x9 (hardcover) • $26.95
ISBN: 978-1-938905-68-1

Road Trip Eats: 101 Ya Gotta Eat Here Places Across Kentucky with Recipes
272 pages • 6x9 (hardcover) • $24.95
ISBN: 978-1-938905-98-9